‖‖ ‖ ‖‖‖‖‖‖ ‖ ‖ ‖ ‖‖‖‖‖‖‖‖‖‖‖‖ ‖ ‖‖

⟨⟩ **W9-AEN-292**

D43
2005

A Teaching Assistant's Guide to Primary Education

A Teaching Assistant's Guide to Primary Education has been specially written for teaching assistants taking up posts in primary schools who are working at NVQ Levels 2 and 3 of the National Occupational Standards of Teaching Assistants.

This jargon-free book covers every area of primary education that teaching assistants will need to know about, including:

- An overview of primary education
- The role of the teaching assistant
- The information you will need
- The knowledge, skills and qualities you will need
- The children
- Learning and teaching
- The curriculum
- Managing behaviour
- Providing for all children
- Evaluation and record-keeping
- Your professional development

Written by someone who knows primary education inside-out, this accessible introduction to the teaching assistant's role in the primary school contains lots of case studies based on real-life scenarios and should be essential reading.

Joan Dean OBE is a former teacher, college lecturer, primary school headteacher, primary schools adviser and chief inspector. She has lectured in many parts of Britain and abroad, and has written numerous books on different aspects of education.

A Teaching Assistant's Guide to Primary Education

Joan Dean

Routledge
Taylor & Francis Group

LONDON AND NEW YORK

LIBRARY
NSCC, STRAIT AREA CAMPUS
226 REEVES ST.
PORT HAWKESBURY, NS B9A 2A2 CANADA

First published 2005
by Routledge
2 Park Square, Milton Park, Abingdon, Oxon OX14 4RN

Simultaneously published in the USA and Canada
by Routledge
270 Madison Avenue, New York, NY 10016

Routledge is an imprint of the Taylor & Francis Group

© 2005 Joan Dean

Typeset in Bembo and Gill Sans by
Florence Production Ltd, Stoodleigh, Devon
Printed and bound in Great Britain by
TJ International Ltd, Padstow, Cornwall

All rights reserved. No part of this book may be reprinted or
reproduced or utilised in any form or by any electronic,
mechanical, or other means, now known or hereafter
invented, including photocopying and recording, or in any
information storage or retrieval system, without permission in
writing from the publishers.

British Library Cataloguing in Publication Data
A catalogue record for this book is available from the British Library

Library of Congress Cataloging in Publication Data
A catalog record for this book has been requested

ISBN 0–415–35234–7

Contents

Glossary

ADHD   Attention Deficit Hyperactivity Disorder.

Aided schools   Church schools for which the church pays a proportion of the expenses and the LEA pays the rest.

Code of Practice   A code laid down by the DfES stating how children with SEN should be provided for.

Concept   An abstract idea, such as the classification of groups by numbers, shapes or colours.

Controlled schools   Church schools for which the LEA pays all expenses.

Core subjects   National Curriculum subjects of English, mathematics and science.

DfES   Department for Education and Skills.

Equal opportunities   Each school is required to have a policy that supports the idea that all pupils should have equal access to education.

Foundation schools   Schools which were grant-maintained under the last Conservative government and independent of LEAs are now again responsible to their LEA.

Foundation Stage   The pre-school stage of education, comprising nursery classes and schools and the reception class.

Foundation subjects   National Curriculum subjects other than English, mathematics and science.

GCSE   General Certificate of Secondary Education – examinations taken at the age of 16 by all pupils.

ICT   Information and communication technology.

IEP   Individual education plan for children with SEN.

Key Stages   Education is divided into Key Stages. Key Stages 1 and 2 include education at the primary stage and Key Stages 3 and 4 are secondary school stages.

Kinaesthetic   Concerning movement.

LEA   Local Education Authority.

Levels   The results of the SATs tests and children's performance in all subjects are assessed in levels. The average level at Key Stage 1 is level 2 and at Key Stage 2 the average level is level 4.

Literacy Strategy   Schools must provide an hour each day of literacy work, using a pattern laid down nationally.

LMS   Local management of schools – each school is given a sum of money to meet school expenses. This is controlled by the governors working with the headteacher.

LSAs   Learning support assistants, employed to support a child or children with SEN.

National Curriculum   All maintained schools have to follow the National Curriculum, which lays down what should be taught and learned at each stage of schooling.

NNEB   Nursery Nurses Examination Board.

Numeracy Strategy   Schools must provide an hour each day of work in mathematics using a pattern laid down nationally.

NVQ   National Vocational Qualification.

Ofsted   Office for Standards in Education. Inspectors from Ofsted inspect schools at regular intervals and report on their findings.

PE   Physical education.

PSHE   Personal, social and health education.

QCA   Qualifications and Curriculum Authority, which has overall responsibility for the curriculum and examinations.

RE   Religious education.

SACRE   Standing Advisory Committee for Religious Education – a committee set up in each LEA to oversee RE and to provide an RE syllabus for schools.

SATs   Standard Assessment Tests taken by all children at the ages of 7 and 11.

Schemas   Mental arrangements of ideas.

SDP   School development plan. Each school, working with staff and governors is required to make an SDP for the future each year.

SEN   Special educational needs.

SENCO   Special educational needs coordinator.

STRB   School Teachers' Review Body – the committee that decides upon school teachers' salaries.

TTA   Teacher Training Agency.

Chapter 1

About primary education

If you are a teaching assistant in a primary school or are thinking of becoming one you will need to know something about present-day primary education. You will have memories of your own schooldays and you perhaps have children at this stage and so you may have a good deal of information already, but education tends to be always changing in some respect or other and there is still a good deal to learn.

There are a number of different types of school serving children of primary school age. At the pre-school stage there are nursery schools and nursery classes run by the Local Education Authority (**LEA**) and others run privately. There are also playgroups run by parents. Many nursery classes are attached to primary schools and this can be an advantage in that the child will be partly familiar with the infant school s/he goes on to when reaching the age of 5. Local authority nursery schools are usually led by a qualified teacher and assistants often have the Nursery Nurse Examination Board (**NNEB**) qualification or some other qualification in child-care.

Maintained schools for children of primary school age may be infant schools catering for children from the age of 5 to the age of 7, junior schools catering for 7- to 11-year-olds or primary schools catering for the full range of primary school pupils. In some areas there are first schools catering for children from 5 to 8 or 9 and middle schools catering for children from 8 or 9 to 12 or 13. First and middle schools were developed following the recommendations of the Plowden Report published in 1967. A number of authorities since then have reverted to the former pattern of a break at 11, since this fits better with the organisation of the **National Curriculum**.

Primary schools may be church schools. The Church of England supported schools for children before education was provided nationally and as a result many schools, in villages in particular, are Church of England schools. These are of two kinds. Some are called **aided schools**. Here the local authority pays staff salaries and the running costs of the school, but the church makes a contribution when building is required. Other church schools are called **controlled schools** and in these the LEA pays for everything, but the church has governor representatives as it does in the aided schools. The Catholic Church also has aided schools and there are a small number of Methodist schools and Jewish schools and a very small number of Muslim schools.

Some maintained schools are called **foundation schools**. These schools were grant-maintained under the last Conservative government, that is, they were independent of the LEA and were funded centrally. This changed when the Labour government took over and they are now part of the provision made by local government, but have foundation governors.

The work of schools is controlled by the Department for Education and Skills (**DfES**) at national level and by the LEA at local level. The Secretary of State for Education is responsible for:

- establishing and keeping under review the National Curriculum;
- approval of the provision and closure of schools;
- determining the standards for school buildings;
- approval of schemes for local financial management of schools;
- providing for teacher training;
- providing for the inspection of schools;
- seeing that LEAs provide an adequate system of education in their areas.

The LEA is responsible for:

- providing schools to give all children in their area appropriate educational opportunities;
- ensuring that the National Curriculum is implemented;
- establishing schemes for local financial management of schools;
- supporting schools that are in difficulties;
- appointing governors to represent the local authority;
- publishing admission arrangements for schools;
- ensuring that pupils attend school regularly.

There are three stages in primary education. The first stage is called the **Foundation Stage** and the remaining two are called **Key Stages** 1 and 2. The stages and year groups are as follows:

Foundation stage	Age 3–4 years	
	Age 4–5 years	Reception, Year R
Key Stage 1	Age 5–6 years	Year 1
	Age 6–7 years	Year 2
Key Stage 2	Age 7–8 years	Year 3
	Age 8–9 years	Year 4
	Age 9–10 years	Year 5
	Age 10–11 years	Year 6

Children take national tests in English and mathematics at the end of Key Stage 2 and tests in English, mathematics and science at the end of Key Stage 3. These tests are known as **SATs** – Standard Assessment Tests. The school must inform parents of the results of these tests. The results are given in **levels** 1–5 in primary schools. At Key Stage 1 the expected level is level 2 but some children may not achieve this and those with special educational needs (**SEN**) may only be working towards level 1. Other children may achieve levels 3 or 4. At Key Stage 2 the expected level is level 4 and here again some children may not achieve this and others may achieve a higher level. The results of Key Stage 2 tests are sent on to the secondary schools, which are expected to provide additional coaching for children who did not achieve level 4 at the end of their primary schooling. Teachers also have to assess children according to these levels and this information, too, must be given to parents.

Schools must meet for at least 380 half-day sessions in each school year. The school day should be divided into two sessions with a break between them. The Secretary of State recommends the following weekly lengths of lesson time for pupils:

- twenty-one hours for pupils aged 5–7 years;
- twenty-three and a half hours for pupils aged 8–11 years.

School governors

Every school has its own body of governors. This is a group of people who give their time voluntarily to support the work of the school. Some are representatives of the LEA, some are elected to represent the teachers and some the support staff, some are elected representatives of the parents of children currently in the school, some, in church schools, represent the church, some, in foundation schools, are foundation governors and some are co-opted as representatives of the wider community. Governors normally serve for a period of four years but in many cases serve more than one term of office. The headteacher can choose whether or not to be a governor but attends all governors' meetings whether s/he is a governor or not.

Case study 1.1

Josie was considering whether to apply for the post of teaching assistant in her local school. She talked to various people about it, including friends, one of whom was a school governor there. She had heard of governors but didn't know what they did. She asked her friend, Jim, to tell her about being a governor and to explain what they did.

He explained that they had a general responsibility for the school, while the head and senior staff had responsibility for day-to-day management. They made the policies that set a framework for the decisions taken by the headteacher and staff. They dealt with appeals and grievances from the staff and with the exclusion of children who behaved unacceptably. They were also responsible for the appointment of the headteacher and deputy headteacher.

They were expected to check that their policies and decisions were being carried out and that monitoring of work by the headteacher and senior staff was taking place. They might be described as being a critical friend for the headteacher and staff, providing both pressure and support. The governing body of a school provided a sort of public accountability for the spending of public money.

Josie thanked him for all this information. She thought that being a governor sounded quite demanding.

A more detailed view of the work of governors suggests that they are responsible for the following:

- Monitoring the work of the school. Governors need to see the school in action from time to time and study the results of tests.
- Making, ratifying and reviewing school policies. Some policies will be drawn up by governors, others will be drawn up by the headteacher and staff or be a joint effort between staff and governors. Governors are legally required to have policies for the following:
  - procedures for admission and appeals
  - aims and objectives of the school
  - attendance, behaviour and pupil conduct
  - charging and remissions for school activities, such as visits
  - child protection
  - complaints
  - curriculum
  - discipline and behaviour of pupils, including steps to prevent all forms of bullying
  - employment, including staff discipline, pay, competence and grievances
  - **equal opportunities**
  - health education
  - pupils' records and reports
  - religious education (**RE**) and collective worship
  - sex education (primary schools need this only if they decide to include it in the curriculum)
  - special educational needs (SEN).

  Parents are entitled to see any of these policies on request.
- Overseeing the school's finances. Under the scheme for local management of schools (**LMS**) the headteacher and governors have responsibility for deciding how to spend the money available for staff, other resources, premises and other needs.
- Overseeing the state of the premises, equipment and grounds.
- Overseeing the curriculum and the teaching and learning programme. Governors are responsible for seeing that the National Curriculum is taught and in primary schools for making a decision, normally in consultation with parents, about whether sex education shall be part of the curriculum.
- Ensuring that RE is taught and that there is daily collective worship. Parents may withdraw their children from both these activities and from sex education if they wish but the school is still responsible for them.
- Ensuring that provision is made for pupils with SEN.

- Working with the headteacher and staff to formulate a school development plan (**SDP**). Schools must each year draw up a plan for future development, normally covering a period of about three years, and update this annually.
- Ensuring there is good discipline in the school. Governors should have a behaviour policy that sets out what behaviour is expected of pupils. They should be informed of any exclusions for unacceptable behaviour and will be involved when these are permanent exclusions and where parents appeal against the exclusion.
- Seeing that there are equal opportunities for pupils of both sexes, ethnic minority pupils, different social groups and pupils with disabilities. Governors should be made aware of any diferences in performance between different groups of pupils, for example between boys and girls, or between children from different ethnic groups, and encourage improvement for the weaker groups.
- Receiving and acting upon inspection reports. Schools are inspected at regular intervals and once the report is received governors with the headteacher and staff are responsible for drawing up and implementing an action plan. Parents must be sent a summary of the report.
- Setting annual targets for the school. Governors are required to set targets for the percentage of pupils attaining level 4 or above in English and mathematics at Key Stage 2.
- Providing an annual report to parents on the work of the school and governing body. The annual report should be discussed at an annual meeting of parents. It must contain information about pupil performance against the targets set.
- Providing a home/school agreement. All schools should have an agreement signed by parents, a representative of the school and, with older children, by the pupil.
- Marketing the school to the local community. Schools are financed according to the number of pupils they attract. It is therefore essential that the school considers how to present itself to the local community.

Parents

Parents are obliged, by law, to see that their children are educated, either by sending them to school or by some other means, perhaps teaching them at home. In practice, very few parents opt for this.

Schools have a legal obligation to provide parents with certain information about the progress their children are making each school year, starting with the reception class. For all children it must include:

- brief comments on the subjects studied as part of the school curriculum, particularly English, mathematics and science, noting the child's strengths and achievements and suggesting areas where there needs to be improvement;
- details of the child's overall progress with comments on behaviour and attitudes to school and the contribution s/he has made to the life of the school and any special achievements;
- information about the arrangements for parents to come to the school to discuss the report and the child's progress with his or her teachers;
- a summary of the child's attendance record.

The Local Education Authority (LEA)

The task of the LEA is to see that the law on education is complied with by providing schools for the children of people living within its area. The finance for this provision is partly provided by government and partly by the local council tax. A large proportion of this money is passed on to the schools on the basis of the number of pupils on the roll and the schools then have to meet running costs, including staff salaries. The LEA is responsible for school premises but, in the case of church-aided schools, part of the money for premises is raised by the church.

Each LEA will have an Education Committee composed of locally elected councillors and teacher and church representatives. This committee appoints a Chief Education Officer or Director of Education to run the education service and a number of officers to support him or her in this work.

Each LEA also appoints a number of inspectors or advisers whose task is to monitor and support the work of schools. They are sometimes called inspectors and sometimes advisers, but the work they do is roughly the same. The members of this service will provide advice and training opportunities for teachers as new developments come along and advice to headteachers and governors on making appointments to the teaching staff of the school. LEAs also provide training for governors and governing bodies need to encourage their members to take advantage of these courses.

LEAs also employ a number of educational psychologists who support schools in various ways but particularly in helping them to provide for children who have learning or behaviour problems. A psychologist may test such children and advise schools on how best to provide for them. S/he will also advise the Authority on the need for extra resources in certain cases, such as learning support assistants (**LSAs**) for such children, or particular equipment needed.

Another group of LEA employees are the education welfare officers – social workers who are responsible for seeing that all children in the appropriate age group attend school and for helping to sort out any difficulties.

The LEA is also responsible for providing home-to-school transport where this is needed.

The Department for Education and Skills (DfES)

The DfES has overall responsibility for education and makes the laws governing it. It has to compete with other departments for funding for education, much of which is then transferred to LEAs. It has a number of semi-autonomous bodies that help in the process of overseeing the education service. The Qualifications and Curriculum Authority (**QCA**) is responsible for curriculum and examinations. The Office for Standards in Education (**Ofsted**) is responsible for school inspections and for keeping the Department informed about the state of education in the schools. The Teacher Training Agency (**TTA**) oversees teacher training and the School Teachers' Review Body (**STRB**) recommends the levels of teacher salaries. The Department also commissions research into the education system from time to time.

Chapter 2

The role of the teaching assistant

Teaching assistants have a variety of titles – classroom assistant, learning support assistant (LSA), special needs assistant and probably others, but they are all concerned with supporting teachers and children. Usually as a teaching assistant in a primary school, you will work with just one classroom teacher, but sometimes your services may be shared by more than one classroom teacher. LSAs or special needs assistants are employed to provide support for a particular child or children who have SEN, but, if you have particular responsibility for helping the learning of one or more children, you should be prepared to help other children from time to time so that the child in question does not feel too singled out. You also want to avoid the child becoming too dependent on you and your help should always involve him or her in making decisions about the work in hand.

Your work with children

Working with only one teacher makes it easier for you and the teacher to work as a team, agreeing your planning together each day and supporting each other. Where you need to work with more than one teacher, it is still important that you are a team in which you share planning and discuss what has happened together. It is just a matter of finding time to do this, which isn't always easy!

In a team you need to agree what is to be done and build a climate of trust between you and the teacher and between you and the children. You need to be clear about the boundaries of your responsibility and when you need to refer something to the teacher. When you are new to the job you may need a good deal of support from the teacher while learning how to work with the children to get the best results. You may also learn a good deal from watching the teacher.

The teacher benefits from having an assistant to work with, not least because having another adult in the classroom means that there is another pair of hands to share the work and this increases adult/child contact. The teacher can delegate routine tasks, such as looking after resources, photocopying, collecting money and so on. The children benefit because there is another person to help them with their work, to listen to them and to help their learning. Good schools and teachers try to discover all the skills and abilities that teaching assistants bring to their work and to make use of them for the benefit of the children.

Your work may include hearing children read and recording their progress, explaining something the teacher has said or the words on a worksheet or in a textbook to a child who has not understood, discussing difficulties with a child, reading a story to a small group, playing learning games with children, working with children with disabilities who need special equipment for their work, mounting wall displays of children's work, looking after resources, helping children as they use computers and recording their progress and supporting many other activities. It is a very varied and interesting job.

Some suggestions about assessing what you can offer

If you are thinking of applying for a post as a teaching assistant, you need to think about what skills you might bring to the job. What experience have you of being with children? Being a parent is, of course, a very valuable qualification, but you may have had other contact with children, such as doing volunteer work in a school. Can you type? Are you familiar with computers? Do you play the piano or other musical instrument? Have you any hobbies that might be of interest? Are you interested in dance or drama or a particular sport? Have you travelled widely? Have you had experience in a previous job that might be relevant? Schools can make use of many different skills and types of knowledge and you need to make the most of what you can offer.

Listening to children will be an important part of your work. Children are helped to learn by putting their ideas into words and a busy teacher in a large class has too little time to listen to children as much as s/he would like. You are another person to listen to children and you need to encourage children to talk about their work so that you get to know how much they understand and the gaps in their knowledge.

Children with special educational needs

If you are employed as an LSA, your main task will be to help the children in the class with SEN. The school will have a special educational needs coordinator (**SENCO**) who will help you to get to know the particular problems of these children and your task will often be one of explaining work set by the teacher in much more simple terms, perhaps breaking it up into shorter stages and asking questions to find out how much the child in question has understood. You may also need to explore any background knowledge involved that the child may or may not possess. Your teacher will probably expect you to help any other children who appear to be having difficulties. It is a good idea to check first whether s/he would like you to do this.

Those with SEN will each have an individual education plan (**IEP**) and you will be instrumental in helping the children in question to meet the targets in the plan. You may also be involved in the making of IEPs for children whose special needs have just been noted and for the revising of the IEPs for others.

You will need to keep the class teacher as well as the SENCO informed about the progress of the children with SEN and any others whom you have been helping.

Case study 2.1

Raksha was a teaching assistant in a Year I class, working with Margaret, her class teacher. The children were working on phonics in the literacy period and Margaret asked Raksha to work with a group of four children who were not getting on very well with this work. She had time to plan this work overnight and was ready with ideas about how she would work.

Raksha started by talking about rhymes with the children, asking them what nursery rhymes they knew and talking about the words in them that rhymed. She then gave them another nursery rhyme and asked them to identify the rhyming words. The next task was to listen to four words and say which two rhymed. Next she gave them a word at a time and asked them to find another word that rhymed with it.

This all went well and she decided to move on to the next task she had prepared. This was an 'odd one out' game in which she gave them four words with one that had a different sound to the others. For example, she gave them 'bun, fun, pun and can' and they were able, quite easily, to identify 'can' as the odd one out. She then asked them what made the odd word different from the others, giving them practice in recognising sounds within words. After some practice at this, she asked them if they could think of some similar questions.

Finally, she went through the alphabet with them asking for the sound and name of each letter. They did well at this, too, and she was able to report to the teacher that they had all shown that they knew the sound of all the single letters and could usually recognise these in simple three-letter words.

Care of resources

Another set of tasks that the teacher may like you to help with is the care and organisation of the resources of the classroom. Resources quickly get out of place as children use them and the teacher may want you to see that everything is back in its right place at the end of the day. The use and care of resources is eased if they are in suitable containers where this is appropriate and are clearly labelled so that children can see where things go.

You may also be involved in the preparation of materials for the work of the class. The teacher may want you to add to the resources available, for example by making new worksheets or photocopying existing material so that more is available. S/he may want you to prepare materials for the children, perhaps cutting up paper for painting or laminating work-card material. Children may like to help you with tasks like sharpening pencils or replacing items in their proper place.

Mounting and putting up displays of children's work may be part of your role. The teacher will tell you how s/he wants work displayed and will probably want to choose what should be displayed. Sometimes the teacher will want you to put up the best work and at other times s/he may want to encourage less able children by putting up work that is less good. Displays shouldn't be left up for too long, so this is a recurring task, but the results can be very satisfying. In some schools classes take it in turns to display work in the corridors or hall as well as in the classroom.

Learning in nursery and reception

An important way of learning in the nursery class and reception is through play. Children learn many things in the course of their play and they learn particularly from the materials available to them. For example, children playing with water can learn about volume measures by having litre jugs available and seeing how many cups they can fill from the jug. They learn about weight by weighing things and seeing which things are heavier than others. They can be asked to find who is the tallest child in the class simply by comparing heights. Counting comes into these activities. They learn about colour from the opportunities they get to paint, perhaps learning how to mix paint and discovering which colours mixed together make other colours.

Children also learn social skills from their play. This may involve taking turns or asking permission to join in an activity. It can involve being helpful to other children. Sometimes children will explain things to each other and talk about what they are doing and you need to do all you can to encourage such interchanges.

In all these activities the teacher or teaching assistant helps children to learn by the materials that are available and by questioning and discussion about what they are doing. Learning is enhanced by adult suggestions and sometimes by the adult joining in the play. Adults also help children to deal fairly with each other and be ready to help other people. We noted earlier that children learn by talking about something and play situations offer good opportunities for talk, both with other children and with adults.

Another activity that provides incidental learning is looking at books with an adult and talking about the words and the pictures. Reading a story to a small group offers an opportunity to introduce new words and ideas and to point out some of the printed letters and words. You also may be asked to read a story to the class.

A further task in which you may be involved if you work in the nursery or with a reception class is that of welcoming new children to the school and helping to make them feel at home. School is a big change from home, especially for children who have not had experience in a nursery class or school. The child is one among many with a limited number of adults. Many things will be strange. Words like classroom and cloakroom may be new. Getting on with other children may be difficult at first. Children need to be helped to cope with all these new things, even if they have had experience in a nursery or playgroup, and you will be in a position to reassure them and help them come to terms with new people and a new environment.

Children sometimes need personal attention during a lesson. A child may be feeling unwell, have an accident or hurt him- or herself and the teacher will want you to care for the child while s/he deals with the rest of the class. The school may have somewhere to take such a child and it is as well to find out when you first start your job what you can do in such circumstances. First-aid knowledge may be useful to you.

In some schools teaching assistants will be expected to take a turn at playground duty. The school will have some rules about behaviour in the playground and your task will be to see that children play amicably together, not getting into fights or quarrelling, and avoiding dangerous games or games that interfere with other people. You may be able to help children who seem to be isolated from the groups playing together to join in.

Case study 2.2

Clarissa, the class teacher with whom Jessie was working as a teaching assistant, suggested that it would be very useful to reflect together each day on what had happened. She suggested that she and Jessie should try to find a time at the end of each day to go over the events of the day and tell each other about their experience. They would each think about the work they had done with children during the day and consider what they had learned and its implications for the next day's work. Jessie would report to Clarissa on what she had noticed in the parts of the lesson where Clarissa led the work. Sometimes she saw things that Clarissa had missed, from which both of them could learn, and Clarissa often asked Jessie to look out for particular things and especially the reactions of particular children. Clarissa also talked with Jessie about what she had done, congratulating her on various pieces of work that had been very successful. She also made suggestions about better ways of tackling some things. Jessie found these discussions very helpful. They gave her ideas for the next day's work and helped her gradually to develop skill in working with children. They also made her feel part of a team with Clarissa.

Record keeping

You will also need to get into the habit of keeping records of the progress of the children with whom you work. Your teacher or the SENCO will give you an idea of the kinds of records that will be helpful to them as well as to you and the children. Such records will be part of your reflection at the end of the day and you will need to share them with the teacher concerned. They may be records of how well different children read and how much they read, of computer use and the skills children demonstrated, of progress in understanding how to do something in mathematics and of anything else that indicates progress or persisting difficulties.

Questions for consideration

1   What do I know about primary education and the role of the teaching assistant?
2   What could I bring to the role?
3   Why do I want a post of this kind?
4   Am I clear about the things I would be responsible for?
5   How could I find out more about the work?
6   Would I be interested in a post as an LSA, helping children with SEN?
7   Would I be more interested in a post with nursery school children or would I prefer one with older children?

Chapter 3

The information you will need

The information you will need before starting the job

When you make an application for the post, you should be given full details of what will be required of you. The information sent to you should also have details of your hours of work and salary. There should be a job description and some indication of the kind of person the school is hoping to appoint, the sorts of experience they are looking for and the kinds of qualifications and skills they are seeking. They will be looking for someone who enjoys being with children and it will be something of an advantage to have been a parent. They will certainly want someone with good English and numeracy skills, and will be looking for **GCSE**s or similar qualifications in these subjects.

The information sent to you will give details of how to apply for the post, will specify the references wanted and will ask for information about your background and qualifications, and why you think you would be suitable. In the light of this, a small number of candidates will be called for interview, usually with the head-teacher and usually the teacher of the class with whom you would be working if appointed, or the SENCO if you are applying for an LSA post. After everyone has been interviewed, the successful candidate will usually be called back and offered the job. Sometimes a school will invite candidates separately for interview and write to the successful person later.

There should be good opportunities on the day of the interview to get to know a number of things about the school. You will probably be taken round the school so that you can get an idea of what it is like and you will meet the teacher with whom you will be working and hear a bit about the children in his or her class. If you are applying for an LSA post, you will have the opportunity to meet the SENCO, who will also be involved in the interview and will tell you something about the children with whom you will be working if you are appointed. You may also get to meet other teaching assistants or LSAs and there may be a senior assistant who will be responsible for your induction.

Case study 3.1

Melanie had been looking for a job with hours that allowed her to spend time with her children ever since her youngest child had started school. She was therefore more than interested when her children brought home a newsletter from their school advertising a teaching assistant's post. It sounded like just the job she had been hoping for.

She remembered that her friend Vicky was already a teaching assistant at the school, so she phoned her to ask what was entailed in the job. Vicky said that for nearly two years she had been a classroom assistant with a Year 1 class and that she thoroughly enjoyed the work and was sure that Melanie would like it too. The class she would be with was a Year 2 and the class teacher was a good one who would make her teaching assistant very welcome.

Melanie then went on to ask Vicky how she spent her days. Vicky said that her class teacher wrote up her plans for the day in advance and gave them to Vicky to read before she went home. Vicky then planned what she might do with one of the groups with which the teacher wanted her to work. Sometimes this would be playing a game or reading a story or helping children with the work the teacher had set. She was responsible for hearing each child read twice a week and had to record this, reporting progress to the teacher.

Vicky also did jobs around the classroom, cutting up paper, photocopying, setting out paints, keeping resources in order and arranging them for the children. She also helped to supervise the children when they changed for **PE** and took a turn at playground duty.

Melanie was reassured by all this and decided that she would definitely apply for the post.

Some suggestions for getting information

It is a good idea to find out all you can about the school and about primary education before applying for a teaching assistant post. Have any of your neighbours children at the school? What do they like about it and what do they dislike? How do they feel their children are doing there? Do the children like it? Your local newspaper will often have reports about schools in the area and the public library should have copies of any inspection reports on the school.

Your local library will also have books on education and you may like to look for *The Effective Primary School Classroom* and *Organising Learning in the Primary School Classroom* (3rd edition). These are both by Joan Dean and published by RoutledgeFalmer. They are written for primary school teachers but have much in them that is relevant to teaching assistants.

The information you will need before you start work

Once you have been appointed you will probably be invited to visit the school to find out more about the nature of the work you will be doing. Ideally, the school should have a teaching assistant's file with all the information you are likely to need, but it is likely that it will be given to you in a more piecemeal fashion. You need to know your way around the school, so you might ask if they have a plan you could use to begin with. You need to know something about the school ethos and aims, the pattern of the school day – assembly, registration, playtimes and lunch hours, the use of names, any dress code, car parking and lunch arrangements, and any health and safety requirements. You should be told about any staff meetings and in-service days to which you will be invited.

You need to know something of how you will be expected to work with the class teacher or the SENCO. What particular tasks will you be expected to do and is there anything you can do to prepare for the work in advance?

Your class teacher will have some rules for children's behaviour in the classroom, such as no talking while the teacher is talking, though they may not be articulated as clearly as that. You can ask the teacher about what s/he rewards and how s/he deals with misbehaviour. There will be school procedures about this and the teacher may have some additional procedures of his or her own. You will want to know what you may and may not do in working with the children. What should you do if a child is rude, swears at you or misbehaves? If a child asks you if s/he can go to the toilet, can you say 'yes' or should you refer to the teacher?

You are also likely to have contact with parents who may approach you about their children from time to time. It is important to know what is confidential information about the children and the school and what may be shared with parents and you need to check carefully with your teacher what you may say to parents and what is confidential information. In any case of doubt, you should refer them to the teacher, or, if more appropriate, to the headteacher.

The information you will need in your first term

As you settle into the work, you will find many other things you need to know. You will be involved in the literacy and numeracy hours each day whether you are an LSA or a more general assistant. Teachers are now asked to spend an hour each day on each of these subjects. The time is broken up into starting activities with the whole class, which might be work on mental arithmetic in mathematics or work on a shared text in English. The lesson then goes on to look at new material or revision of previous material in mathematics, or work on phonics or spelling and punctuation or different types of writing in English, followed by a period in which children work individually or in groups on the work that has been covered in class, and you will be asked to help them in various ways. In both subjects the lesson should end with a plenary session in which the learning is reviewed.

You will also want to know about the National Curriculum. This covers all subjects, except RE and lays down the material that should be taught at each level. RE is covered by church and local authority schemes, although a national voluntary code to guide local authorities is being prepared. The school should have a scheme of work in each subject, based on the National Curriculum or the local RE scheme, and you will gradually become familiar with these as you work with the teacher.

There should be an opportunity each day to plan with the class teacher or the SENCO or both. S/he may produce a written plan and share it with you beforehand so that you have some time to prepare or you may have to snatch what time you can to share ideas each day. You also need regular meetings to evaluate the work you have both been doing. How did a particular lesson go and what did the group or individuals you were working with get from it? What have you learned from the experience? What does this suggest would be a good idea for the next step?

Another area of knowledge with which you need to become familiar as soon as possible is knowledge about the children with whom you will be working. The SENCO and/or your class teacher will tell you about them and you will find it helpful to look at their records as well as observing the children and working with them. The children with SEN in particular will, in many cases, have an IEP setting out targets for the child and you need to be familiar with this whether or not you are an LSA. Teachers should also set targets for other children and you will be contributing to helping them achieve these.

If you are an LSA you will need to know something about the *Code of Practice* for children with SEN. This sets out the stages of assessing children's special needs. Initially the class teacher notes that a child is having difficulty with learning. S/he makes a plan for the child and puts it into practice. If the child does not make progress, the school can ask for an assessment by a psychologist, who will test the child and make recommendations to the school. As a result an IEP will be made. If there is still little progress, the school or the parents, who should be involved at all stages, can ask for a statutory assessment to be made by the LEA. This will involve further testing by a psychologist and, if the child's difficulties appear to warrant it, a Statement of SEN will be made, which specifies the help the child should receive. This may involve the services of an LSA. A further IEP is then made and the case is reviewed regularly.

The school will have a number of policies, some of which will involve you. There will be a health and safety policy, which will affect subjects like technology and PE as well as the general supervision of children. You also need to know what to do in the case of accident or fire. Another policy that may affect you is the child protection policy. Children come to trust assistants and it is possible that a child may tell you of abuse of some kind. In this case you should tell the teacher, who should report it to the headteacher. There will also be a policy about giving equal opportunities to children. Teachers need to see that boys and girls, children from ethnic minorities and children with SEN are treated equally, or, if not equally, are given equivalent attention and care.

Each year the school has to make a development plan, setting out targets for the year and the way they will be addressed. You need to know about this, because the teachers you will be working with will be planning towards the aims set out in the SDP and will want your support in achieving them. You don't need to know the detail of the plan, just the elements with which your teacher is concerned.

Case study 3.2

Eva started work as a teaching assistant in September. She really enjoyed the work and quickly made friends with other teaching assistants and with her class teacher, Indira. She learned from the other teaching assistants about the school's performance management programme. This involved being observed annually at work in the classroom by Jane, the deputy head. She would be asked to provide a statement about her work, identifying areas in which she felt she needed further training and areas in which she felt comfortable. Her class teacher would also be asked for a report on her work. She would then be interviewed by the deputy head about her work and have the opportunity to discuss how she felt she was doing. Jane was a very kind person and very supportive. She said she had received good reports about Indira and congratulated her on her first year's work. They then went on to discuss the areas where Eva felt she was having difficulty. She felt that she lacked knowledge of the way children developed and learned and she needed to learn a lot more about ways of tackling difficult children who tended to play her up if the class teacher allowed it. They talked about this and Jane made some suggestions that Eva found helpful. Jane also suggested that she might now consider undertaking some training at the local college and work towards a National Vocational Qualification (**NVQ**). Eva liked this idea and Jane told her how she could get on a suitable course.

Eva had been a bit alarmed at the idea of the performance management interview but in practice found it helpful and practical.

_____

This all sounds quite a lot of information, but you will get to know
it slowly as bits of it affect your work. There should be lots of
opportunities for you to ask questions of teachers and other assistants as well as documents concerning these various issues. Probably
the most important information is that which concerns the children and it will take time to get to know them as individuals. This
is probably the most rewarding part of the job.

Questions for consideration

1   If I am applying for a job as an assistant, have I all the inform-
     ation I need? How can I obtain more?

2   If I am about to start work as an assistant, have I all the
     information I need? What opportunities are there to find out
     what I need to know? Do I know the pattern of the school
     day? Am I clear what will be expected of me?

3   If I am now in post as an assistant, am I familiar with the
     school's main aims?

4   Am I clear about what I should do and when I should consult
     the teacher or the SENCO? Am I familiar with the teacher's
     rules for classroom behaviour?

5   Do I have regular opportunities to discuss the work planned
     with the class teacher and/or the SENCO?

6   If I am working as an LSA, am I familiar with the stages of
     assessment for children with SEN?

7   Am I getting to know the children well and are they beginning
     to trust me?

8   What do I know about school policies and the current SDP?

Chapter 4

The qualities, knowledge, skills and attitudes needed

If you are thinking of applying for a post as a teaching assistant or LSA, you need to think carefully about what you could bring to such a post. If you are already in post, this chapter should be useful for self-evaluation, helping you to think about the contribution you can make to the work of the school.

Personal qualities

Anyone interviewing candidates for an assistant's post will be first of all concerned to appoint someone who is the kind of person who will really enjoy working with children. Such a person will like children and it will be an advantage to have had some contact with children. The interviewers will be looking for someone sensitive, warm, caring and enthusiastic who respects other people and makes good relationships easily with adults and children. You also need to be calm and patient and have an understanding of children's needs. A good sense of humour is helpful, for children appreciate someone who is fun to be with. You will need to be well organised and a good time-keeper to do this job well, especially if you also have a busy home life.

A school will want someone who is willing to learn and evaluate the effect of his or her work, always seeking better ways of doing things. They will be looking for a mature person likely to be able to work with others in a team, respecting differences and making a good personal contribution. You also need to know your own strengths and weaknesses.

The knowledge you will need

At the start you will need some knowledge of primary education – the names of the year groups, for example. As time goes on, you will need some knowledge of the National Curriculum, the subjects that are taught at each stage and the arrangements for the literacy and numeracy programmes. You need to know that there are two Key Stages for primary education: Key Stage 1, which is tested at the age of 7 by the SATs, and Key Stage 2, which is tested at age 11. There is also a Key Stage 3 in the secondary school.

You will need a good knowledge of English and elementary mathematics and some knowledge of other subjects, although there will obviously be the opportunity to learn along with the children. Knowledge of computers will also be helpful, because you will probably be helping children using them.

Another area in which you need knowledge is that of knowing what is confidential and what may be passed on to parents and children. You need to be very careful about this when you first start and be ready to ask whether information that comes your way is confidential.

Skills

When you first start as a teaching assistant you need to spend time observing the teacher and the children. Note the physical setting and how the resources are arranged and used and how the teacher manages the class. It can be helpful to look at work on display since this gives you an idea of what the children can do.

Some suggestions for observation

Observe the children and their reactions to the teacher and to each other. Do some children always volunteer to answer questions and others rarely put their hands up? Do boys put their hands up more often than girls? What sort of language does the teacher use and does this change if children appear not to understand? What sorts of questions are asked and how does the teacher respond to the answers? The information you gain from such observation will be useful to you in working with the children.

Another important skill is the ability to make good relationships with children. You need to show that you are really interested in them and listen carefully to what they have to say, maintaining eye contact and smiling and being ready to follow up ideas. Treat them with the same respect you would show to an adult and try not to talk down to them, although of course you will need to use language they understand, particularly with the younger children. Demonstrate that you have high expectations of them by telling them that you expect them to be able to work well without interrupting each other and that you look forward to seeing some good work. Be sympathetic to a child in difficulty and do your best to help.

Teaching assistants need many of the skills of a teacher. You need to develop a good understanding of the children with whom you work, so that you can identify the best way to help them. This means assessing where they are in their learning and looking for how best to help them to take the next step forward. The teacher should help you to decide what you need to record when you hear reading or work with a child with learning difficulties. Your records will be shared by the teacher and the SENCO in some cases, but you need to make records for your own benefit so that you can plan ahead. These are skills you will develop as you learn on the job and are helped by the class teacher and the SENCO.

Surveys of children's opinions of a good teacher show that they value highly a teacher's ability to explain things. They will also value this in a teaching assistant. You will often be in the position to help a child understand what the teacher said, particularly if you are an LSA, and you need to develop this skill to a high level.

You need to be a good listener, to try to understand children's points of view, recognising that they each have their own thoughts and feelings that they may or may not choose to share with you. Good listening involves not only hearing what is said but also showing that you are listening by your body language, leaning towards the person, maintaining eye contact and using appropriate facial expressions. You also need to look for the children's body language. Are they showing that they are enthusiastic and keen or bored and tired? Can you tell from looking at a child whether s/he has understood what you have been saying? Fidgeting and yawning are often a sign of boredom and a sign that you need to do something different to capture their attention.

Body language is also important when you are speaking. It can add emphasis to what you are saying. Where there is a conflict between what a person is saying and the manner in which it is said, most people will react to the non-verbal communication and get a mixed message. Children react quickly to body language from a very early age because it is their way of reading a situation at a stage when they have limited language. This will be particularly important with younger children and children with learning difficulties.

Another skill that you will need is the ability to ask questions and follow them up when necessary. Some questioning will be a matter of checking what children know and understand. You may also be asking questions to revise previous work before introducing something new. It is important to think about the way you respond to children's answers, especially if they are wrong. Be encouraging about good answers and tactful about incorrect ones. If you are scathing when an answer is wrong you will find that children will be less and less inclined to answer. You also need to ask some open-ended questions, which make children really think and which will give you the chance to help them develop ideas. You may then want to ask questions to encourage the child to develop the ideas further. It helps to pause a little after asking a question to give children a chance to think about it, particularly when asking open-ended questions. The children should be encouraged to ask questions themselves and you can do this by praising good questions when they are asked.

A further particular skill you need to develop is the ability to praise contingently – that is to be specific in praising a child for good work or good behaviour, saying something like 'That is a very good piece of writing, Jamie. I like the way you have started off by describing the scene and it was good to see you looking up the words you couldn't spell in the dictionary.' It is important to use praise a good deal because children need encouragement and it is a good rule to praise much more often than you criticise. Criticism should be made very tactfully so that the child does not feel that you are criticising him or her as a person and is led to see how to avoid evoking this particular criticism again. It makes criticism more acceptable if you can link it with praise for some other aspect of their work.

Case study 4.1

Jenny had applied for a teaching assistant's job at her local primary school. The headteacher and the class teacher who interviewed her were interested in what knowledge and skills she had to offer the school and asked her detailed questions about her previous employment. She explained that she had trained as a secretary and had good shorthand and typing skills. After two secretarial jobs she had worked for four years as office manager for a transport firm. She left when her children were born and now wanted a job that would fit in with her home responsibilities. They were interested in this experience and thought that it could be useful in the classroom. They were impressed by her, feeling that she had much to offer, and therefore offered her the job, which she accepted.

When she started the job, Margery, the class teacher, talked to her about what she had done as office manager and concluded that she would make a good job of looking after and organising resources. Jenny was happy to do this and soon had a rather chaotic collection of materials sorted out.

They then talked about ways in which she could use her typing skills to support classroom work. She could make worksheets and lists, which would be helpful, but in particular she could be helpful to Ahmed, an intelligent child who had great difficulty reading and writing. Margery suggested that, using large type, Jenny could copy out stories and other material dictated by him. These could then be used by him as reading material. She could note the words he could read and work with him in helping him to learn to write them as well as to spell other words he knew but couldn't spell.

This worked well and Ahmed made good progress. Jenny felt that her skills were being well used and that she was really being helpful.

Attitudes

Finally, the people appointing a teaching assistant will be looking for certain attitudes to the work. They will want a person who is positive and doesn't give up when things are difficult. This means persisting with a child who has great difficulty in learning or behaving well and looking for the good things in each child.

They will be hoping to appoint someone who is willing to work hard and learn about the job, and who is ready to undertake training and learn from others – a committed person who enjoys seeing children learn and make progress.

It will be particularly important to be reflective about your work, thinking over what has happened in the classroom each day, noting what has gone well and asking if a different approach to some work would have been more productive, then planning for the next day's work, taking into account what you have learned today. Ideally, you should do this with your teacher or SENCO, but it may be difficult to find time for this every day. You need to be self-critical but not so critical that you lose self-esteem.

Questions for consideration

1   What qualities could I bring to the work of a teaching assistant?

2   What do I need to know before applying for a teaching assistant's post. What will I need to know when I am in the job? How can I find out what I need to know?

3   What skills have I which could be useful in the classroom? What new skills will I need to develop? How can I best do this?

4   What attitudes will help me to do this job well?

Chapter 5

The children

Children develop in many ways through the primary school years and knowledge of the stages of development can be helpful in setting realistic expectations of the children you work with and in planning work for them. They develop physically, personally and socially, in the use of language, intellectually and emotionally and they also go through various stages of development in their play. In observing children you can look out for the stages of development they have reached in different aspects of maturity as they grow and this will help you to judge what is appropriate for them.

Physical development

Babies learn to move in different ways and, as they grow, they learn to crawl and then to walk. Young children use movement to gain the things they want. They learn to pick things up and manipulate them and these skills develop into the ability to draw, write and make things, skills that continue to develop and become more refined through the primary school years. In play they move in many different ways and gain skill in controlling their movements. PE in school should help this.

Growth during the primary school years is fairly rapid and the head and brain, in particular, grow faster than the rest of the body, which doesn't catch up until the person is adult. At age 5, the brain and head are about 80 per cent of adult size and at age 7 this increases to 90 per cent, whereas the body is almost at the halfway mark.

Generally speaking, girls are more advanced than boys in some aspects of growth during the primary years and they tend to reach puberty earlier. Boys catch up during adolescence.

The left hemisphere of the brain is concerned with language and the right hemisphere with spatial relationships. The left hemisphere of the brain is more advanced in girls and in boys the right hemisphere is more developed, which probably accounts for the fact that girls tend to be ahead of boys in English and the arts, and boys ahead of girls in mathematics, science and technology.

Personal and social development

Children begin to form ideas about themselves from a very early age. The self-concept is important in creating a child's attitudes to learning. Children who think well of themselves come to new learning with a positive attitude and the belief that with effort they can succeed. Sometimes this belief is unrealistic and you may need to reassure them and persuade them to further effort. They are not aware at the early stage of the idea that people may have different abilities and they tend not to distinguish between the effects of effort and ability. Where a child does not think well of him- or herself you need to praise as much as you can and encourage the child to have a go at things, reassuring him or her if the result is not as good as s/he would like.

Case study 5.1

Johnny was the only child of parents who had had to make their own way from a rather disadvantaged background. They had high expectations for their child that they felt he failed dismally to live up to. From a very early stage he grew accustomed to comments like 'Is that the best you can do?' and 'Can't you do anything right?' By the time he started school he had concluded that he was just dim and would never be any good at anything.

The teaching assistant in the reception class was Elspeth, who soon realised that he had a very poor self-image. The class teacher, June, agreed with her and they decided that they must do all they could to change his view of himself to a more positive one. They agreed to praise him all they could and to make this praise contingent, so that he could look at his work and enjoy a feeling of satisfaction. This was difficult at first because he was reluctant to try anything new and was convinced that he couldn't do things. Elspeth made a point of showing any good work to the children round about saying 'Look what Johnny has done

– isn't it good?' June tried to select his work for display whenever possible and they both singled him out to do jobs around the classroom and then praised him for doing them. Gradually, he became more ready to try new things and less inclined to say 'I can't do that.' They also made a point of praising him to his parents, because they guessed that they were the cause of the poor self-image. Jennifer wrote to them from time to time, saying how well he was doing, and they were surprised but pleased by this.

At the parents' evening Jennifer talked to Johnny's parents about his poor self-image and explained what she and Elspeth were doing and that it was important to get Johnny to feel ready to try new things and help him to feel good about himself. She said she hoped they would go along with this and try to praise him at home. They were a bit shocked by this but thought it over when they got home and decided to try to be less critical and more encouraging.

By the time Johnny moved into Year 1 he was much more confident and showed signs of being quite a bright boy.

Young children tend to see the world only from their own point of view. This is very evident in the nursery and is still at least partly the case until about the age of 7. You need to take opportunities to talk about how other people see things and encourage children to think about this. As children grow older they begin to be able to see from points of view other than their own and become more sensitive to other people. They need gradually to learn to cooperate and to recognise how someone else is feeling and be sympathetic towards the other person. This needs to be encouraged by talking about how others see things and praising cooperation when you see it. They need to develop social competence and skills such as the ability to form and maintain satisfying relationships, through readiness to cooperate, negotiate, take turns and share with others, as well as other communication and social skills.

It is important that both you and the teacher convey the idea that you have high expectations of children. It is very easy to convey the opposite without realising it, particularly when dealing with children with SEN. A comment like 'That's very good, for you' or the equivalent conveys the idea that you didn't expect much.

Children also need to develop the ability and confidence to be self-critical, to express themselves clearly and succinctly and to learn how to behave appropriately and responsibly in different situations. As children grow older they begin to compare their performance with that of other children and this may lead to a lack of confidence and unwillingness to express ideas and have a try at something. You need to be reassuring in such cases, finding things you can praise and encourage and particularly encouraging effort. Make it clear that you believe in the child's ability and will support him or her.

Young children start by exploring the environment and discovering the world around. They gradually become more social but still tend to see the world as revolving around themselves. In adapting to any environment and to new ideas children take in new information and try to relate it to what they already know. This may mean making adjustments to previously held ideas. By the time they are 7 years old they begin to be able to see from another's point of view, but their thinking is still tied to action. It isn't until children reach the age of about 11, and in some cases much later, that they can really think abstractly.

Children also need to learn acceptable ways of behaving and the values that govern society. Some of this learning takes place before children come to school or nursery, but there is a great deal for them to learn at school. They need to learn the importance of telling the truth, of polite behaviour, polite ways of asking for things, the need to thank other people and show appreciation and ways of greeting people. The adults need to model desirable behaviour, treating children as well as each other with respect.

Children tend to like other children who are friendly and sociable and the ability to get on with peers is an important part of learning at every stage. You need to encourage children to be helpful to each other and to listen to what other children have to say. Good cooperative behaviour should be praised. It is particularly important to work at developing good social competence and behaviour in children with SEN, especially those with disabilities that hinder communication, such as poor sight or hearing. It can be a good idea to ask a child who has good social skills and is sympathetic to befriend such a child and help him or her join in with the play of other children.

Growing up in the type of society that now exists in Britain, where people may be of other races and other social backgrounds, children need to be encouraged to respect the worth of other individuals and groups, have tolerance towards them and see people as individuals with different backgrounds and ways of looking at things that may be as equally valid as their own.

Part of growing up is the acceptance of one's gender. Research suggests that boys and girls are treated differently from a very early age and schools need to be conscious of the need to create equal opportunities for them. This does not mean working in exactly the same way with boys and girls. Boys from an early stage will tend to choose different toys and activities to those chosen by girls. Boys tend to play differently from girls and respond better to work that involves practical skills and physical activity. Teachers have been found to interact more with boys than girls, perhaps because boys tend to be more demanding. They also tend to attribute poor performance in boys to lack of motivation and poor performance in girls to lack of ability. Girls tend to like school more than boys and to make better progress, particularly in English.

Children in school are part of a child culture that will influence them and be something they have to learn to live with. They will have a shared view of school that helps them to cope with the demands made by adults. There will be demands made to have the right clothes, speak as other children do, do what other children do, watch certain programmes and so on. This becomes increasingly important as children grow older.

Language development

Babies are born able to hear differences between all the possible different speech sounds. This ability disappears quite rapidly as they become attuned to the sounds of their native language. They start to use words somewhere around the age of 12 months. Adults point things out to a child and say what they are called and the child gradually tries to make the same sounds and so learns the names of things in his or her environment.

The next step is to learn the rules that govern the child's native language. In doing this children sometimes make mistakes and say things like 'I runned round the garden' or 'I goed to the shop.' They learn the correct version because parents and others tell them what they should have said and they learn by imitation and reinforcement.

By the time a child comes to nursery school, s/he will have a vocabulary of about a thousand words and will ask lots of questions and usually will have a lot to say. By the time children go to primary school, their vocabulary will probably have increased to something like three or four thousand words and they will soon be developing early literacy skills.

Language is an essential part of social behaviour. Children learn language by listening to other people and talking to other people. Language is also part of the process of thinking. We think in both words and pictures. Young children need to talk out loud about what they are doing, but gradually this becomes the inner speech by which we talk to ourselves, work things out, remember, relate objects to one another and decide what to do. Children also use language to regulate their behaviour.

Talking is a very important part of learning and children should have many opportunities to talk about what they are learning. They need the chance to use language for different purposes – for planning, organising ideas, reporting, working with other people, asking questions, reasoning and evaluating. Group work and paired work is valuable in this context, particularly where it encourages the use of new vocabulary learned earlier in the lesson. You can be very helpful in discussing new words with children and helping them to use them correctly. Dialogue with an adult is a very valuable learning opportunity. By needing to talk to someone else they learn the importance of making things clear to the other person and, when that person is an adult, s/he can help them increase clarity. Errors and mistakes are clues to what the child has not understood.

Another aspect of language is the type of language the children are using. Some schools will have the task of trying to encourage children who have learned a dialect form of language at home to learn and use standard English. This needs to be done very tactfully, because telling a child that what s/he says is wrong may appear to be something of a personal attack and be damaging to self-esteem. Probably the best way of tackling this problem is to say that we say things differently in school, just as we don't swear in school, and to praise the child when s/he uses the more correct form of language, at the same time suggesting that there is nothing wrong in using their everyday language with friends or at home. With older children you can suggest that standard English is more likely to get you a good job when you grow up and is something you will need when you take examinations in the secondary school.

You may also have in your school some children for whom English is not the first language, and who may start school with

very little understanding of what people say to them. Research suggests that such children eventually have an advantage and develop
a greater social sensitivity, because they become very sensitive
to facial expression and non-verbal communication generally. In
dealing with such children you need to use a lot of non-verbal
clues, pointing to things or demonstrating what you want the child
to do. Try to use the same expressions often so that the children
come to recognise them. You may be fortunate enough to have a
bilingual assistant working in your school and this will help.

Intellectual development

Children develop and learn through the experience of interacting
with their environment. This is why provision for young children,
in particular, places great emphasis on the provision of interesting
experiences that they can talk about with adults and with each
other and learn from. Experience is still important with older children and providing appropriate experiences at the right time is very
much part of the teacher's task. Experience gives rise to language
and this helps to establish arrangements of ideas in the child's mind.
These are called **schemas** and, when children encounter a new
idea, they try to relate it to the schemas they already have. It is
like a mental filing system where new ideas lead to a search to see
if they fit a particular slot. Of course, in some cases, particularly
with the younger children, the idea will be completely new and
will lead to the establishment of a new schema. You can help the
filing process by relating new ideas to experiences that have gone
before. This is a process of structuring learning so that it is more
likely to be remembered. The child is thus actively engaged in
constructing knowledge.

Each of us inherits from our parents a level of general intelligence. It used to be thought that this determined a child's intelligence level for life, but later research suggests that intelligence
can be fostered and developed, although some children will be
naturally more intelligent than others. It is probable, too, that there
are a number of different kinds of intelligence. These may include
linguistic and verbal intelligence, logical-mathematical intelligence,
visual and spatial intelligence, which will show itself in ability in
the visual arts, bodily **kinaesthetic** intelligence, which will lead
to ability in physical activity, musical intelligence and interper-
sonal intelligence, which will manifest itself in the ability to make

good social relationships. People can also be intelligent about themselves, having good self-knowledge. Observation of the kind of intelligence each child shows can lead to a better understanding of learning style and the kind of approaches that will benefit each child.

Emotional development

A very important part of children's early experience is their emotional development. Emotional responses are a primitive response to danger and are controlled by a different part of the brain from that which controls rational thinking. Human beings respond emotionally more quickly than they respond intellectually and children have to learn to control their emotional responses and need help with this from parents, teachers and other adults. Research suggests that the ability to manage one's emotions probably plays a larger part in success in life than intellectual ability. A person needs to recognise his or her own emotions and manage them, to be self-aware and able to motivate him- or herself and to recognise emotions in others.

Parents and carers play an important and difficult part in helping children to come to terms with the way they are feeling and this is particularly difficult in the pre-school years when children are very much at the mercy of their emotions and may feel swamped by them. Emotions in one person arouse them in another and you may often be deeply affected by the emotions a child is demonstrating.

A child will also be very sensitive to the way an adult is feeling. If you are depressed or angry or harassed the child will sense this and react, and this may create a problem for you. It is important to appear calm in the face of an emotional outburst on the child's part, even though as an adult you are feeling anything but calm. It may help to discuss the way the child is feeling or distract him or her or leave the child alone to calm down. The ways adults deal with the child's and their own feelings are important sources of learning for the child. Feelings should not be ignored and children should be encouraged to seek better ways of expressing them. Good parents and carers take the child's feelings seriously and talk over disturbing situations. They also need to help children realise that aggression and passivity are non-productive. Children need to be helped to find more useful outlets for aggressive feelings.

Case study 5.2

Rajan was a very angry little boy. He had had temper tantrums from an early age and his parents just hoped he would grow out of them, but, at nearly 7, he was still showing anger quite forcefully. He was often in trouble for fighting and he was not very popular with the other children. When he was having difficulty with his work he would sometimes throw it on the floor or tear it up. He was inclined to lash out when he thought someone had been critical of him and had once attacked a teacher. Punishment had no effect or even the opposite effect because he then became angry about the punishment itself. His parents and class teacher were becoming despairing of ever getting him to behave more reasonably.

The way the school usually coped with this sort of behaviour was to send the child out of the room to somewhere else to cool down. The trouble was that when Rajan was sent out he tried to damage anything within his reach. Barbara, the class teacher, discussed this with Elsa, her teaching assistant, and suggested that when Rajan became angry Elsa should take him to a quiet room and try to calm him by discussing what had made him so angry.

Elsa did this and worked to get him to see other points of view on the incident that had enraged him. She also talked about his need to learn to control his anger by substituting calm thoughts for angry ones and they talked together about how he could have done this in the current circumstances. They also talked about other occasions when he had been angry and discussed what he might have done instead of lashing out. She stressed that people who get angry frequently lose friends and don't have anyone to play with. She suggested that he practise behaviour that other children would like, such as discussing problems rather than fighting and smiling and saying nice things to other people.

Rajan responded quite well to these suggestions and Elsa made an arrangement with him to meet every week and discuss how he was getting on. They would keep a chart of the number of occasions when he lost his temper and he would try to make these fewer each week. Each time, they discussed these occasions and talked about what he might have done instead. This worked and he gradually became more controlled and less of a problem.

Children project their own feelings on to others and if you are working with a child you may need to ask yourself about the feelings the child is arousing in you. Your tolerance level is linked to your own capacity to manage disturbing feelings.

Research suggests that parents discuss emotions with their daughters more often than with their sons and use more emotional words in talking to girls than to boys. Girls tend to have better language ability and this helps them to articulate their feelings and so come to terms with them. Girls are often better at reading other people's feelings. This suggests that perhaps school staff should often talk to boys about their feelings in order to help them come to terms with them. Research also suggests that people prone to anger are more likely to die young than smokers!

Good teachers and assistants also try to take account of children's emotional reactions and feelings. In some classes the teacher holds what is known as 'circle time', in which children sit in a circle and talk about how they felt in different situations and discuss how they might react when they felt angry or upset and the effect of these reactions on others. In particular, such work tries to help children to manage feelings of anger and unhappiness by thinking of different ways of reacting. Children also consider how they might recognise other people's feelings and help them by reacting sympathetically. Circle time gives children a chance to discuss such

---

Acquiring knowledge of child development

It is important to get to know as much as you can about the way children develop and learn. If you are a parent you will already have considerable knowledge about this from watching your own children. You may also have the opportunity to hear about the children of friends and relatives. As a teaching assistant, you will be constantly aware of the importance of this knowledge and you should look out for books that might help, as well as observing children and talking to parents and teachers. A valuable book that covers the ground well is *A Teaching Assistant's Guide to Child Development and Psychology in the Classroom*. It is written by Susan Bentham and is published by RoutledgeFalmer.

issues as feeling they are not coping if they ask for help, or feeling that school life should be fair all the time or blaming other people when they feel unhappy. Children need to learn to be competent emotionally. This means being able to recognise the feelings of others and being sensitive to them. Children who are able to do this tend to be more popular with their peer group. Circle time discussions also provide an opportunity to discuss bullying and how to deal with it. Listening to others is stressed, as is giving everyone the opportunity to say what s/he wants. As an assistant you can also have discussions with children on similar topics.

The development of play

Young children play naturally with everything that comes to hand. It is part of their exploration of the environment and is an important part of their learning. The baby handles everything that is available, attempting to discover what it is like by squeezing it, pulling it, tasting it and so on and in doing this gradually discovers something of the nature of the world around. The small child continues to explore in this way and this is often a worry to parents because it can be full of dangers. Gradually, children begin to play alongside others without necessarily involving them or being involved with them. This develops into play with others.

Children also invent and imagine in play. A child gradually begins to play at being other people and in doing this starts to discover what people are like, playing out the activities seen in the home and the neighbourhood, such as house cleaning, shopping and visits to the doctor or relations, and in the process learns a great deal about the subject of the play as well as coming to terms with some of the situations involved.

Language is an important part of the learning that goes with play. Young children will practise the language they hear their elders using and by joining in the play with other children. You can help language development by introducing new words and ways of speaking.

Children also use play and drawing to help them come to terms with the way they are feeling about things. A child who has gone through an upsetting situation may play out similar situations with dolls or a teddy bear or may draw pictures of what happened. This is valuable for the child's emotional development and may provide opportunities to talk about what happened.

When young children start school, whether this is in a nursery school or class or in a reception group, the staff will work to extend their language by the material provided for play, since children will talk about what is there and new language can be introduced in the context of play. Play will be used to introduce the beginnings of mathematics and science. Children playing with water, sand and similar materials will discover relationships between weight, size and volume, for example, and, if there is an adult available to talk to them about what they are doing, this will become part of their background knowledge.

This early use of play gradually changes to the use of play to provide practice. For example, infant classes will often have a shop available as part of their mathematics work and children will learn about money and counting by playing at buying and selling. Games will also be used to help children learn and remember basic number facts or the beginnings of reading. At a later stage a game like Scrabble will give excellent practice in spelling and in mental arithmetic.

Children also learn a great deal socially in the course of play. Young children have to learn to share and take turns and this is an important part of learning at the pre-school and reception class stage. Older children learn skills useful for adult life, such as playing to rules, influencing others and knowing how to join in, how far to go and so on. Play at all stages is concerned with getting on with other people.

Play with good adult support gives children the opportunity to develop their ideas and skills, to think creatively and imaginatively and express themselves, to negotiate and cooperate with others as they play and to make sense of their world. It helps language development and is an important element in learning for young children.

Questions for consideration

1   What can the children I work with do physically? Are some of them more advanced than others? What is the evidence for thinking this?

2   What social skills do the children have? What can I do to help them develop these?

Library, Nova Scotia Community College

3 What is the range of language ability among the children with whom I work? What evidence should I look for to assess this? What language skills should I be helping them develop?

4 What different kinds of intelligence do the children show? Can I use this information to help them learn?

5 How sensitive am I to children's feelings? Am I able to react appropriately to the way a child is feeling?

6 What stages of play are the children I work with at now? How well do they work together in their play? What play opportunities do they need?

Chapter 6

Learning and teaching

The subjects to be studied at school are set out in the National Curriculum, which defines a Foundation Stage for pre-school education and sets out the subjects to be studied at each subsequent stage. There are the **core subjects** of English, mathematics and science, and the **foundation subjects** of art and design, design and technology, geography, history, information and communication technology (**ICT**), music, PE and personal, social and health education (**PSHE**). The foundation subjects have nothing to do with the Foundation Stage of education. RE is also compulsory, but is not yet part of the National Curriculum. Schools work instead to a syllabus laid down by the LEA. Each school should have its own schemes of work, setting out the elements of the National Curriculum to be studied at each stage.

This chapter is called learning and teaching, rather than teaching and learning, in order to emphasise the fact that children are learning all the time from their experience, whether they are taught or not. Teaching extends this natural learning into new areas.

Children start to learn from the moment they are born and possibly even before that. Everything that happens to them is a source of learning and parents are very important in this process. Very young children learn principally in four ways. They learn through the experiences of observing and exploring their environment. They learn through play, some of it as part of the process of exploration. They learn by watching and imitating the people around them and they learn by talking to other people. These ways of learning are at the heart of the work of nursery schools and they remain important in the primary school.

When we think we tend to do so in a mixture of words and pictures. The pictures are things we have experienced and the words help us to sort out the experience. With this mixture of words and pictures you can work out inside your head what will happen if you do something. You don't actually have to do it to find out. You can also think over what has happened, think what to do next and go over something that went wrong. Children have to learn to do this and they are helped by talking about what they are learning.

The home and the local environment provide experiences to explore through which children learn, helped by interaction with their parents and others. Parents and nursery schools and classes provide opportunities for the child to explore through the materials and toys they provide for play and through the opportunities they provide. Language as it develops plays an important part in this learning and research suggests that the adults' role in talking and listening to children is crucial. Adults need to be sympathetic listeners, sensitive to the message the child is trying to convey and skilled in responding. Parents provide many opportunities to learn through talking in the course of normal daily activities, such as cooking, cleaning, visiting the supermarket and gardening. In all these situations they talk about what is happening and point out things to the child and try to answer the questions that arise.

Talking about what is happening with children and encouraging them to talk about it is important. Very young children talk about what they are doing as they do it. This gives you clues about what they are thinking and the talk out loud eventually becomes the inner speech we all use in talking to ourselves. Children also use talk to assert themselves, to establish relationships, to try to get what they want and to express their ideas.

Adults also talk of things that are going to happen and things that have happened and from this children learn to talk about the past and the future and about objects that are not present. You can encourage this by asking questions about experiences they have had and questions about what they are going to do.

It is also important to get across the idea that effort is necessary for achievement. Young children tend not to have an understanding of the relationship between ability and effort and it is only when they are older that they appreciate that different people bring different levels of ability to a task. It is important at all stages to stress the need to try hard.

Types of learning

Learning at all stages depends upon experience. The child needs to match language to the experience and understands what others are saying in terms of the experience s/he can bring to the situation. If you talk about something outside the child's experience then you need to match what you are saying with examples that the child has experienced. If, for example, you are reading a story about an elephant, pictures may help the child to imagine what an elephant looks like, but you need to compare its size with something the child has experienced if s/he is to get a good idea of what an elephant may be like.

Learning from experience

First-hand experience plays an important part in children's learning at every stage and is as relevant in school as it is at home. Teachers take trouble to bring things into the classroom for children to observe and you can do this too. The teacher may take them on visits to see things outside the school, using this as a basis for their learning. They will only be able to learn from your words or the words of the teacher if they can match the words from their own experience and this is especially relevant while the children are very young and therefore very limited in experience.

Concept development

Another important part of learning is **concept** development. A concept is an idea. It may be something as simple as a colour or the idea that three-sided shapes are called triangles or it may be something as complex as the idea that things are either living, non-living or once living. Children develop concepts of being good or naughty, or kind or unkind, from an early age. They learn about these ideas from the way parents and others react to their behaviour and the labels people give to it. They learn about the world around them by observing and experimenting and learning the labels that adults give to things around them. A child may learn the word 'dog' and for a time may call all four-legged animals 'dog', but then gradually learn to differentiate the characteristics of dogs from those of other four-legged animals, such as cats. They learn to count and have to learn that the number words (concepts) can be applied to anything that can be counted. They learn that some things are called heavy and others light, some things long and others short, and some things round or square or pink or blue. All these ideas are concepts. Much of this learning takes place incidentally in the home but in school concept development will be the subject of more specific work, such as learning what is meant by addition, subtraction, multiplication and division and how to use these operations.

How children learn

The traditional idea of learning at school is one of transmission of knowledge by the teacher to the pupils and then testing to see whether the learning has taken place. While this way of learning has a necessary place, it does not accord with what we know about the way children learn. As we saw in Chapter 5 and earlier in this chapter, we all construct our learning from our experience. A child will take what you or the teacher says and what the teacher shows the class and the experience you make available to the child and fit this into his or her mental organisation of knowledge or schema. This may be different for each child and it is important to check on the way the children are understanding the work in hand.

Learning how to learn

Teach children to structure what they know so that it is available when it is needed. Try suggesting ideas and structures that will help them to remember what they are learning. Suggest ways in which they can do their own structuring by grouping things together and arranging them in order. Look for ways of helping them to learn that they are likely to remember. For example, if you are helping them to remember how to spell words ending in 'ing', give them examples of pairs of words such as 'love, loving, dance, dancing', and ask them to see if they can work out the rule for adding 'ing' to words ending with 'e'. This will help them to remember the rule more effectively than if they had simply been told about it.

It is important to help children to be positive about learning. This means using descriptive praise frequently and using situations in which children make mistakes to suggest positive ideas for avoiding the mistakes in future, or to suggest ways in which work could be improved, trying when possible to combine this kind of help with praising correct answers. You need to demonstrate that you have high hopes for everyone, teaching children that everyone makes mistakes and that this is how you learn. Work to enhance children's self-esteem and pay particular attention to helping to raise the sights of children who appear to have low self-esteem. Talk about the things they can do and ways in which they have been successful when they become depressed about their progress. Avoid making comparisons of the work of different children, although it may be helpful sometimes to call attention to those children who are behaving well and getting on with their work.

Case study 6.1

Eddie was an 8-year-old with SEN who found written work very difficult. He not only found difficulty with spelling and punctuation, but with thinking of anything to say in writing, although he was happy to talk.

Lynne, who was his LSA, established a good relationship with him and he was ready to talk freely to her.

One playtime when she was on duty, he started to talk to her about a robin's nest in his garden at home. He described how he had watched the female bird sitting on the eggs and how the male bird brought her food. He put out crumbs for them and watched the male collect them and take them to the nest. Next day he came up to her showing some excitement, to tell her that the eggs had hatched and there were five baby birds in the nest.

Lynne listened to all this sympathetically and it struck her that this would be something he could write about with enthusiasm. She suggested to the class teacher that, when they got to the individual work stage of the literacy hour next day, Eddie should be encouraged to write about the nest. The class teacher agreed and Eddie started quite enthusiastically to try to write about what he had seen. He wrote more than he had ever done before and although there were spelling mistakes the writing was vivid and interesting. Lynne and the class teacher praised him and suggested that he read what he had written to the class. He was thrilled to do this and managed it quite well, with very few hesitations.

Learning styles

When we learn we do not simply take in information, we process it into the schemas we looked at in Chapter 5. If it is completely new, we form a new schema for it. If it can be associated with existing schemas, we fit it in with what we know. Different children have different ways of dealing with new information and forming schemas and so have different ways of approaching learning. Some children learn best by seeing things. They use observation and reading to help their learning. Others learn well through listening carefully and going over what they have heard in their heads in order to commit it to memory. Doing things actively is the style that some children find helps them best and this is often the case with boys. In fact, active learning in which you move or handle things is helpful to most children at the primary stage. Even at this stage, some children tend to be more analytical and process what they are learning by grouping ideas and organising them into a logical pattern that they can remember. It is helpful to try to assess how different children learn best, particularly if you regularly work with a small group of children, or particular individuals whom you can get to know really well. This kind of information can be a useful guide to you as to the best way of helping them remember what they are learning.

Aspects of learning

The phrase 'learning something' has a lot of different meanings. It may mean the concept development we met earlier in this chapter. It may also involve information that has to be memorised, such as number bonds, multiplication tables or spellings. Some learning involves skills – the ability to add up, subtract, multiply and divide or the ability to draw and paint, or write fluently or move in certain ways, catch a ball, run swiftly and so on. Nearly all learning involves language and children need to learn the meaning of words and how to use them.

Concept development requires a number of experiences of the concept to form the necessary schemas. This is the most complex part of learning and concepts may change and develop as the child grows. Some information needs to be memorised and children need help with this. If the information can be grouped in some way or associated with something the child already knows it is easier to remember. The spelling of new words is more likely to be remembered if children are encouraged to associate them with words they can already spell. Number bonds to ten can be associated with your fingers, which give you an easy way of calculating. Multiplication tables are best learned practically using counters or objects and grouping them, so that children can form images of different multiples, although this becomes too complex for the tables of larger numbers. New language coming with new learning can be helped by recording it for future reference and giving children plenty of opportunity to use the new words.

Case study 6.2

Children often learn things at school that their teachers didn't intend. Jean was a teaching assistant and she found that the children in the Year 4 class with which she was working were very ready to talk to her about all sorts of things. As she was walking home one day two of the girls joined her and started to talk about school. They told her that the subjects they liked best were art and PE, but they weren't very important. The important subjects were English and maths. One of the children said she didn't like maths much and tried to work slowly because if you worked fast you just got more of the same boring sums to do.

They said that they thought the teacher liked boys better than girls because she asked more boys than girls to answer questions and talked more to boys than girls about their work. They thought it was good that they were white because the white children were cleverer than the black children and the teacher liked them better.

Jean was rather shocked by these revelations and wondered whether the teacher realised that she was giving these impressions. She thought she ought to somehow make her aware of what the children thought, especially if the views of these two girls were widespread. Frances, her teacher, had said she would like Jean to observe her and both see what she could learn from the observation and also note anything that she thought Frances was missing. Jean decided that she would watch out for any evidence of the things the children had said so that she could tell Frances about them. She found that it was certainly the case that the teacher asked boys more questions because they tended to put their hands up to answer more, but she couldn't see much evidence that she liked the white children better than the others. It was true that maths and English were stressed a great deal, but this was probably right. Overall, the hidden curriculum that the children had revealed seemed to be partly justified.

Learning in groups

Children at the primary stage of education need opportunities to talk over what they are learning in order to make it part of their thinking. They can also learn from each other and so schools plan some work in pairs or groups. Sometimes these are ability groups and sometimes mixed ability groups. Mixed ability groups are better for learning by talking, because the less able will learn from the more able and a class teacher may deliberately structure groups to allow for this. Ability groups can be useful for differentiating work according to ability, particularly in mathematics, but being in a low ability group can be very discouraging and sometimes leads to teachers having expectations that are too low. The teacher needs to be very conscious of this problem and do all s/he can to overcome it.

Group work is often planned for a kind of problem-solving in which a group or pair of children are given a task to talk over and to come up with conclusions about. They might, for example, be asked to read a rather difficult passage and discuss what it means, or plan a particular aspect of work on a project, such as one on their village, making suggestions about how they could study this. Groups might then feed back to the whole class and get further suggestions for carrying out their ideas. You may be asked to work with such a group, helping them to share ideas, seeing that everyone is given a chance to contribute and helping them to sum up in preparation for presenting their ideas to the class.

Questions for consideration

1   What different kinds of learning are the children in the class I work with experiencing? What are they learning from first-hand experience? Is there a hidden curriculum?

2   What part does children talking together play in their learning? How effectively do they use opportunities to talk together?

3   Do I listen well to children? What do I learn from this?

4   What can I contribute to their learning of concepts?

5   How can I best help children to organise what they know so that they remember it?

6   What have I learned about the learning style of individual children?

7   How often do I praise children? What do I praise them for?

Chapter 7

The Foundation Stage

All schools have to follow the National Curriculum, which sets out what should be taught at the different Key Stages. The Foundation Stage applies to children in nursery schools or classes and to the reception class. Key Stage 1 applies to 5–7-year-olds in Years 1 and 2, Key Stage 2 to 7–11-year-olds in Years 3–6 and the later Key Stages 3 and 4 to the secondary school. English, mathematics and science are regarded as core subjects and other subjects as foundation subjects, except for RE, which is not yet part of the National Curriculum, although schools must teach it. You need to be familiar with the parts of the National Curriculum that are relevant to the children you work with, so that you can contribute to their learning.

The Foundation Stage was introduced in September 2000 as a statutory phase for 3-, 4- and 5-year-olds in playgroups, nurseries and reception classes. Attendance at the early stages is voluntary but a child must attend school from the beginning of the term after his or her fifth birthday.

The Foundation Stage is intended to provide secure foundations for later learning. It provides opportunities to identify and address any difficulties and there may be children with SEN who require particular help and support. The curriculum at this stage is implemented mainly through play activities. The development of play was described in Chapter 5.

Effective early years education requires a relevant curriculum and an appreciation that children develop rapidly during the early years – physically, intellectually, emotionally and socially. All the children need to feel secure and valued and you need to try to find out what children already know and can do when they come into the group and build upon this, talking with parents about what their children do at home. There should be a rich, stimulating and well-planned environment with many of the activities planned by the adults, but there should also be opportunities for children to plan their own activities, with teachers and assistants observing and responding appropriately and engaging children in learning. The resources provided determine the learning that takes place. These should be varied and include both indoor and outdoor play opportunities. Activities should usually include the opportunity to count, look at books and play at writing.

If play is to provide for this kind of learning it must be carefully planned and children's learning as they play must be observed and noted so that there can be planning for further learning. As you work with the children you should look for opportunities for their learning that you can help to develop and encourage. You will gradually start to get ideas about how to stimulate learning through play.

Part of the planning for play is the creation of an environment in which there are many opportunities for children to try activities, investigate, create and make, talk about what they are doing and develop their language skills and learn to work cooperatively with others, taking turns and sharing. The national body responsible for curriculum, the QCA, defines curriculum at this stage as 'everything children do, see, hear or feel in their setting, both planned and unplanned'. The QCA has defined six areas of learning for this stage. They are: personal, social and emotional development; communication, language and literacy; mathematical development; knowledge and understanding of the world; physical development; and creative development.

Personal, social and emotional development

This area involves the development of children's self-confidence and self-esteem and their ability to make relationships, negotiate with others and accommodate them. They also need to learn that there must be rules about many things when a number of people are together. For example, there may be rules about how many children can play in a particular area of the room or the things that children can do and the places where they may go and you will need to help the children to keep to these rules. Good provision should help children to develop a positive sense of themselves and the ability to manage the way they feel.

There is also a need to help children to look after themselves and become independent. The attitude of the adults towards the children is very important here and it needs to be encouraging and deal positively with any conflicts or difficulties that arise. This area of development is the basis for future learning and for happy and successful living.

Communication, language and literacy

An important part of children's learning at this stage is the ability to carry on conversations with other children and adults, and this is where you come in. Children need to be encouraged to talk about what they are doing and to communicate in their play, gradually extending their vocabulary and ability to listen carefully, responding to what they have heard with relevant comment or questions. You may be able to introduce new words or suggest ideas for their play. They should learn to express themselves clearly, using language to organise their thinking, ideas, feelings and recall of events. It is important to listen to them carefully and encourage them. They should be introduced to books and stories and encouraged to talk about them and learn that print carries meaning and that what is said can be written. There should be frequent opportunities to hear stories told or read aloud and much discussion of them. Children's names should be written for them and they should be encouraged to recognise and perhaps write their own names. The older children in the nursery or playgroup should be encouraged to try writing and learn to make the letter shapes and talk about them.

In the reception class there will be many opportunities for reading words on labels about the classroom and for copying writing written by you or the teacher at the child's dictation beneath a child's drawing. Children will learn to write their names and gradually learn to write a number of common words. By the end of the reception stage children will begin to write in sentences and build words from a growing knowledge of letter sounds.

Mathematical development

Children will be encouraged to use numbers to count things in the environment and will learn to recognise common shapes and colours. Numbers should be displayed in the classroom – perhaps a number ladder, which can be used to play at helping a toy to climb the steps with children counting – and children should learn to recognise the numerals from 1 to 10. Work with numbers will also be introduced through stories, songs and games and will be encouraged as part of the children's play. There will be opportunities to add things together as part of play and for counting and experimenting with numbers. Use discussion to introduce words like 'bigger' and 'smaller', 'heavier' and 'lighter', 'over' and 'under' and so on and discuss what they mean. In the reception class children will learn to count reliably and add and subtract numbers up to ten. They will be introduced to the concepts of weight and measurement and time and develop their ideas about shape.

The development of early mathematical concepts

Talk with young children about their experiences of the four rules of number. Have they experience of adding things together? Use an opportunity when children are putting things away and counting them to ask how many coloured pencils there would be if Jimmy had five and Peter had four. Put out the pencils in two piles so that they can be counted. Do they do this by counting pairs of numbers from scratch or can they count on from the first number to get the total? Can they say how many pencils Stephen will have left of a set of ten if he gives five to another child? Can they do this without putting the pencils out and counting them? Could they share out twelve pieces of paper between four children? How many pieces of paper will be needed if the four children in a group need to have two or three pieces each? Use any opportunity that occurs for counting and calculating with real objects and develop this into calculating imaginary objects.

Knowledge and understanding of the world

Children at the Foundation Stage should be encouraged to explore their environment, observing objects and living things, and finding out about them by asking questions. They should be encouraged to look at similarities and differences between things, and ask questions about why things happens and how things work. For example, a group of children might observe what happens when a lump of ice melts and be encouraged to notice that the level of water in the container has risen. You could ask them to guess and then work out how many cups of water or sand are needed to fill a large container. At the reception class stage, children may explore the school grounds, looking at what grows there and the birds and other animals that visit. These activities begin to lay the foundations for later learning in science, design and technology, history and geography.

Physical development

Young children's physical development was discussed in Chapter 5, but here you need to think about how it relates to the activities children are doing at the Foundation Stage. Growth stems from the head downwards and the centre of the body outwards, so that young children may take time to learn to control their feet and legs and the finer muscles of their hands and you may need to think about activities that could help this development. Children at this stage are learning to move safely and with confidence, developing control and coordination of their movements and beginning to show awareness of space, of themselves and of others. They should have plenty of opportunities to be active and develop physical skills. Part of the development involves learning how to use tools, such as scissors and writing implements, and you can help them with this.

Creative development

Children at the Foundation Stage should have good opportunities to explore colour, texture, shape, form and space in two and three dimensions, and respond in a variety of ways to what they see, hear and touch. There should be many opportunities for drawing and painting, making things with clay or plasticine and with scrap materials, and talking about what they have done. You can also encourage experiment. For example, you might encourage them to mix yellow and blue or yellow and red paint to see what happens. There may be cooking activities. There should be opportunities for music-making, dance and role-play using stories they have heard or made up.

Case study 7.1

Liz worked as a teaching assistant in a reception class in an infant school. Maureen, her class teacher, had been working with the children on number bonds to ten and she asked Liz to work with a small group who were not grasping this idea.

Liz started by giving the four children in the group ten counters each and asked them to arrange them in a line and then divide the line into two groups of counters. She then got them to count how many there were in each group. She next asked them to group the counters differently and discover how many different groups they could make. They then wrote down what they had discovered and they practised the sums they had worked out, trying to remember the different possible groupings.

When they had done this for a little while and seemed to be remembering at least some of the pairs of numbers that made ten, she introduced a version of the game Ludo. She had made ten cards, each giving a sum that said $7 + ? = 10$ or $5 + ? = 10$ and so on for all the possible permutations. They then played the game, each child picking up a card when it was his or her go with the task of working out the sum before moving a counter the number of times that was the answer to the question. When a child used a card, s/he placed it blank side upwards on another pile, which the children went on to use when they had worked through the original pile. When they first played the game they were allowed to use the counters to do the calculation, but when they had played it a few times they had to know the answer without help before moving.

Next day, when she felt they had reached a stage where they knew these number bonds, she introduced the idea of working out what other numbers under ten added up to – sums like $3 + 3 = ?$ or $6 + 2 = ?$ or other variations. Once again they worked these out with counters before using another set of cards to play Ludo again.

The children thoroughly enjoyed this activity and soon were able to give the answers without pause for thought.

Baseline assessment

At the end of the Foundation Stage teachers must assess children's progress. This is quite a demanding task for teachers and you may help by discussing your observations of different individuals and how they perform against the criteria for assessment. This provides information against which later development can be assessed and is a form of accountability for the school. It also provides information for future planning of the curriculum for each child and for the whole class. It helps to identify children who have SEN, if these have not already become evident. The assessment will cover language and literacy, including speaking, listening, reading and writing, mathematics, and personal and social development. The results of this assessment should be shared with parents.

Questions for consideration

1 What opportunities for children's learning are available in our classroom? What learning is developing from play activities?

2 What contribution am I making to children's learning? Are there areas where I am finding it difficult to contribute?

3 Are there any children who are finding it difficult to play with other children? What can I do to help them?

4 What have I done to help develop children's language skills?

5 What activities are there that can be used to develop number skills? Am I making the most of these?

6 Am I using encouragement enough? What things have I encouraged in the past two days? Which children have I encouraged? Are there some who seem to need encouragement more than others?

7 What am I doing to encourage creativity? What examples have I seen of children having original ideas about the work they are doing?

Chapter 8

The core subjects

English

The National Curriculum for English

The National Curriculum for English starts with the following statements:

- English is a vital way of communicating in school, in public life and internationally. Literature in English is rich and influential, reflecting the experience of people in many countries and times.
- In studying English pupils develop skills in speaking, listening, reading and writing. It enables them to express themselves creatively and imaginatively and to communicate with others effectively.
- Pupils learn to become enthusiastic and critical readers of stories, poetry and drama as well as non-fiction and media texts.
- The study of English helps pupils understand how language works by looking at its patterns, structures and origins. Using this knowledge pupils can adapt what they say and write to different situations.

The study of English involves the four aspects of speaking, listening, reading and writing. These are not only the subject of study in English lessons but are part of the work in the classroom in all subjects of the curriculum.

The National Curriculum suggests that at the infant school stage (Key Stage 1) pupils should learn to speak clearly, fluently and confidently to different people using clear diction and appropriate intonation, and taking into account the needs of their listeners.

At Key Stage 2 – the junior school stage – pupils should learn to speak with confidence in a range of contexts, adapting their speech so that it is appropriate for different purposes and audiences. They should also be introduced to and encouraged to use standard English when this is appropriate. Standard English refers to the use of appropriate grammar, not accent or dialect. Children should learn how language varies according to situation – they use language differently in talking to their friends and family from the way they use it talking to their headteacher. Some of this can be learned in the context of drama lessons when children try to talk in character roles.

At the infant school stage children should be encouraged to listen actively and with concentration, asking questions to clarify their understanding. Listening will also involve identifying sound patterns in language, such as rhyme, and recognising the sounds that make up spoken words, leading to skill in reading, writing and spelling. These skills should be developed further at the junior school stage and children should become able to identify features of language for specific purposes, e.g. to persuade, instruct or entertain.

At both stages children should learn to use language as part of a group, taking turns in speaking and listening to others. At the junior stage they should be able to relate their contributions to what has gone before, justify their own views, deal with opposing points of view and use different ways to help the group move forward.

The Literacy Strategy

The main part of the work in English takes place as part of what is known as the **Literacy Strategy**, which is a strategy taught to a framework that has now been in existence for some years and has been very successful in improving the teaching of literacy. The *Literacy Framework* suggests that literate primary pupils should:

- read and write with confidence, fluency and understanding;
- be able to orchestrate a full range of reading cues (phonic, graphic, syntactic, contextual) to monitor their reading and correct their own mistakes;
- understand the sound and spelling system and use this to read and spell accurately;
- have fluent and legible handwriting;
- have an interest in words and their meanings and a growing vocabulary;

- know, understand and be able to write in a range of genres in fiction and poetry, and understand and be familiar with some of the ways in which narratives are structured through basic literary ideas of setting, character and plot;
- understand and be able to write a range of non-fiction texts;
- plan, draft, revise and edit their own writing;
- have a suitable technical vocabulary through which to understand and discuss their reading and writing;
- be interested in books, read with enjoyment and evaluate and justify their preferences;
- through reading and writing, develop their powers of imagination, inventiveness and critical awareness.

As part of this strategy, the Literacy Hour takes place every day and is the responsibility of the class teacher, who will look to you to help children with the tasks arising from the class work. The Hour is run in three parts. The programme usually starts with work on a shared text, which lasts for about 10–15 minutes. With younger children this quite often involves reading together from a 'big book' – a book with pages large enough for all the children to see the words. The teacher will focus on their understanding of what is being read, word-building and spelling patterns, punctuation and the structure and organisation of sentences. She will encourage children to use clues for meaning in the text and any pictures as well as encouraging them to try to recognise the words or work out what they are from the letters that compose them. Some of the time the teacher may choose to ask you to carry out this kind of activity with a small group, perhaps of children who need an easier text than that being used by the class.

With older children the teacher may use different texts to help them to recognise the features of different kinds, or genres, of writing, such as poetry, drama or non-fiction, which could be a report of an event or which explains how something happens or how to do something. This may be followed by attempts by the children to write such texts for themselves. This work provides an opportunity for children to work at texts beyond their independent reading level. Again, you may be asked to help with this.

The next stage of the Literacy Hour, which is also planned to take about 15 minutes, is word-level work. With younger children, this will be mainly work with word sounds or phonics and related work on spelling. Research suggests that children's awareness of sounds is associated with success in early independent reading. Children who can recognise rhyme and can map sounds on to letters make better progress. With older children, the second part of the lesson will cover spelling, vocabulary and work on grammar and punctuation. Spelling strategies and rules will be taught, building on from the phonic knowledge acquired earlier.

The third part of the lesson, which should take about 20 minutes, involves guided group work or independent work by children. The teacher may use this time as an opportunity to teach a particular group or ask you to work with a group or an individual while others are working independently or in pairs or small groups. It may include group reading, where a group of children read together from the same text or discuss a topic in groups. It may involve guided writing, where children undertake a writing task, usually one stemming from work earlier in the lesson.

The final 10 minutes of the lesson is a plenary session in which the whole class is brought together to go over and reflect on what has been learned, present work and receive feedback and encouragement.

Speaking

Language gives us the opportunity to recall past events and exchange information. We can think through the possible outcomes of a course of action before taking it and think over what has happened afterwards. It is a tool of the imagination. Language allows children to make relationships with others, to secure cooperation and to coordinate action. Children also use language to direct their own and other people's actions.

Listening

We have seen that listening is an important skill at all stages and you need to encourage children to listen attentively to the teacher, to you and to other children. When you are working with a small group, look for the children who are really listening to what is being said. In discussion afterwards, make encouraging comments to the children who have picked up what was said earlier and refer back to the importance of listening carefully to other people.

Drama will play a part in speaking and listening for children at both stages. They will learn to use language and actions to explore and convey situations, characters and emotions, and explore stories and ideas in plays they devise and script.

Reading

At the infant school stage, the National Curriculum stresses phonic knowledge. Children should be able to hear sounds in words, know the names and sounds of letters of the alphabet, explore rhyme, be able to break words into syllables and recognise that the same sounds may have different spellings. They should also learn to recognise words that occur frequently in written language, particularly those that are not phonetically regular, become familiar with common spelling patterns and recognise parts of words, such as common beginnings and endings. They should also become aware that the order of words in a sentence affects their meaning and be able to work out the sense of a sentence by rereading it or reading ahead.

As they grow older, they should learn to use non-fiction texts, indexes, contents lists, captions and illustrations and develop their understanding of fiction and poetry, expressing preferences and giving reasons for them.

At the junior stage, children learn to use books to find information, learn to distinguish between fact and opinion, recognise different types of text and become familiar with, and develop understanding and appreciation of, a range of fiction, poetry and non-fiction.

Hearing children read

One of your tasks is likely to be hearing children read and recording aspects of this for the class teacher. The teacher will be suggesting what children should attempt to read and you need to think about how you can help children in the process of reading. Sometimes a child will hesitate, unsure of what a word says or making a wrong attempt at it. Give the child time to consider and then, if s/he corrects the first attempt, praise this even if it is not quite right. It can sometimes help to ask the child to read the sentence from the beginning and to try to think of a word that would make sense. Next, see if you can get him or her to break down the word into sounds and syllables, helping with this if necessary. Give the child time to consider and praise if the attempt is right. If s/he still can't get the word, then it makes sense to explain what it says. Try to think of a way to help the child to remember the word and make a note of the problem for the teacher.

Case study 8.1

Julie worked with a Year 4 class and the class teacher often asked her to listen to the reading of a small group of children, checking whether they were understanding what they had read and whether they could make inferences from it. For example, she found a sentence in a story that implied certain things about the main character. It said 'John always rushed at things and sometimes got them wrong. He hated school and the only lesson he really enjoyed was PE.' She asked the group, 'What does this tell you about John?' They made various suggestions. One child suggested that he wasn't very good at school work and liked to be active. Others thought that it sounded as if he was rather careless. Being able to make this kind of inference makes reading fiction much more enjoyable and Julie did her best to help children develop this skill by asking questions about the text and discussing what could be concluded from it. Sometimes when reading a story with a group of children she would stop at an interesting point and ask what they thought would happen next. She also asked questions about the characters in a story. What sort of a person do you think the principal character is? What sort of things would s/he be likely to do? She drew children's attention to the way the author started and ended a story, suggesting that they might learn something from this that they could use in their own writing.

She noted for the teacher how successful these children were at making inferences and also gave her information about how much and how well each child had read. She noted particularly the children who were good at correcting their own mistakes. In addition, she listed the words each child stumbled over, noting these for her own future work with the child. Julie and the teacher agreed that she would consult the teacher if she thought a child was reading something too easy or too difficult and the point at which a child needed to move on to a more difficult book.

Writing

The National Curriculum suggests that children should learn to write for the following purposes:

1   to imagine and explore feelings and ideas, focusing on creative uses of language and how to interest the reader;
2   to inform and explain, focusing on the subject matter and how to convey it in sufficient detail for the reader;
3   to persuade, focusing on how arguments and evidence are built up and the language used to convince the reader;
4   to review and comment on what has been read, seen or heard, focusing on both the topic and the writer's view of it.

Studies and tests suggest that children do less well with writing than with reading, particularly boys, although there may be exceptions. They also find it more difficult. There are four aspects of writing to be learned – the formation of letters, the spelling of words, punctuation and the writing of sentences, leading to the writing of different texts, such as narrative, letters, reports and essays.

Drawing is valuable for pre-school children in helping them to develop the ability to control writing tools. Young children also often do 'pretend' writing – scribbling to look like adult writing. Gradually, children learn to form letters and write their names.

Learning about punctuation

Children need to learn the capital forms of the letters and know when these should be used. Teach them how to write their names and also that new sentences begin with capital letters and end with a full stop. Teach children the trick of listening to a sentence in their heads and noticing whether the voice drops at the end. Try reading aloud to children, asking them to put up their hands when they think you have come to the end of a sentence by listening for the drop in your voice and then get a child to read aloud while the others listen and signal the ends of sentences. They should eventually be able to do this mentally for sentences they have made up.

Drawing letters large in the air or in a tray of sand can sometimes help the child to learn their shapes. The letters you show the child first should be the small letters rather than the capitals. You are likely to be involved in helping children with their writing. At the early stages of school, this may mean helping them form letters. When they are learning joined-up writing it is helpful to practise writing a particular letter by writing a row of them. Tracing over an example of good cursive writing can also be helpful.

Schools vary in the actual shapes of letters that they teach. Some will teach the small letters with a hook for joining so that there is a natural progression to joined-up writing. Other teachers feel that this may be confusing because the letters in the books children read do not have this feature. Both approaches can work successfully.

Getting started

Some children may find it difficult to get started on a piece of writing. It can be useful when a child seems to be having difficulty to ask questions leading him or her to form ideas about what to write. Sometimes you can help a child to remember experiences that would be relevant to the writing concerned and talk about the words that would be useful. Another way you can help younger children with the beginnings of writing is to ask them to draw a story and tell you about what happens. You then write down what they say and read it with them, pointing out the words you have written, and let them copy it. With older children, you can help by talking to them about their ideas for a story and asking questions about the characters and what happens to them. If you have typing skills, it is a good idea with a child who finds writing difficult to get him or her to dictate a story for you to type. You then enlarge the type and give it to him or her to read.

Spelling

Spelling will also be an important topic when you are concerned with writing and you will often be asked how to spell a particular word. It is a good idea to ask the child to have a shot at spelling it out to you. If s/he gets it right it may be helpful to suggest ways of remembering it for the future. This is always a helpful thing to do and you need to try to find something that would fix the word in the child's memory. A word may have some of the letters of the child's name in it and pointing this out may help memory. Tips like 'only one C is necessary' can be useful and if you think enough about it you can make up lots of similar tips for words that are difficult to remember. You can also ask children to do this for themselves and each other. Look for rules of spelling whenever possible – for example, the rule that, after a short vowel, that is, one that says the sound of the letter rather than its name, the consonant that follows is usually doubled.

An important part of learning to spell is memorising the combinations of letters that make up certain sounds that can be put together to make words. It can help to ask children to think of words that sound similar or rhyme and get them to associate the sounds with the letters. Unfortunately, English is not a truly regular language and there are nearly always exceptions to any rule and you will need to talk about these when you talk about spelling rules.

Where you see a mistake in writing, tell the child that there is a mistake in a particular piece of the writing and ask if s/he can spot it and put it right.

Assessment of speaking, reading and writing

Children take tests involving reading at age 7 and 11. These give results in terms of levels of achievement, the average for 7-year-olds being level 2 and for 11-year-olds, level 4. Teachers are also expected to assess children in terms of levels of achievement. Progression will be seen in children's confidence in understanding texts of increasing length that are more complex in language and ideas. Progression will also be seen in the way children respond to a text. In the early stages they will respond in terms of personal preferences and likes and dislikes (levels 1 to 3), but gradually they become able to identify and respond to key features of texts (levels 4 to 6) and show critical appreciation of what has been read (level 6). They also develop the ability to read for information. Your class teacher will welcome information from you about your observation of children's reading skills.

Levels of achievement

At the end of each Key Stage there is a formal assessment by teachers of the level children have reached. The levels to be reached in primary schools are 1 to 5. A number of the more able children will reach level 5. There is also national testing for English and mathematics at age 7 and English, mathematics and science at age 11 (the Standard Assessment Tests or SATs). Teachers have to make judgements about each child's level of achievement based on assessment of speaking and listening, reading and writing skills. The results of the SATs are also given in terms of the levels of achievement. Teachers can then compare each child's test score with their own assessment. Parents should be given information about the levels their child has reached.

At level 1, children might be expected to talk about matters of immediate interest, speaking audibly and providing some detail. They listen to others and usually respond appropriately. In reading, they recognise familiar words in simple texts, use phonic knowledge to build words and respond thoughtfully to what is being read. In writing, children at level 1 should be able to use the formats introduced by the teacher and make reasonable attempts at spelling with some use of full stops and generally legible handwriting.

At level 2 (average level for 7-year-olds), children begin to show confidence in talking and listening, particularly where the topics interest them. They should speak clearly and use a growing vocabulary, showing awareness of listeners on some occasions. They should listen carefully and respond with increasing awareness. In reading, children might be expected to read some material independently and use different strategies to understand what they are reading. In writing, work will be expected to be more structured and organised than at level 1 and show some awareness of the reader. Spelling should begin to improve and show the use of phonic strategies. Work should be well presented with clear handwriting.

At level 3, children are expected to talk and listen confidently in different contexts, exploring and communicating ideas. They begin to adapt what they say to the needs of the listener and are starting to be aware of standard English. They should be reading a range of fiction and non-fiction and understanding what they read. They should also be using their knowledge of the alphabet to locate books and find information. Writing at this level is expected to show imagination and clarity in organising ideas and ability to write in different forms for different purposes. The use of full stops and sentence structure is secure and the ability to punctuate recorded speech is developing. Their ability to spell includes some polysyllabic words. Handwriting should be fluent, joined and legible.

At level 4 (average level for 11-year-olds), children should adapt talk to purpose, developing ideas thoughtfully, describing events and conveying their opinions clearly. They should contribute appropriately to discussion and make contributions that take account of others' views. They should be confident and enthusiastic readers, able to respond to a variety of different texts, including narrative, poetry and reference books, and use inference and deduction in understanding what they read. They are expected to be able to write in a variety of forms, such as narrative, poetry, explanation, diary, notes and so on, using grammatically complex sentences. Spelling should be generally accurate and full stops, capital letters and question marks used correctly. Punctuation should be generally correct.

Children who reach level 5 should be able to talk and listen confidently in a wide range of contexts, including some that are of a formal nature. In discussion, they will pay close attention to what others say, ask questions to develop ideas and make contributions that take account of others' views. They should begin to use standard English in formal situations. In reading, they should be able to retrieve and collate information from a text, show understanding of a range of texts, identifying key points and responding to characters in a story. They should be able to write in a variety of forms, both formal and informal, with confident use of punctuation and spelling. Simple and complex sentences are arranged in paragraphs.

Schools may also use standardised reading tests from time to time to assess how well children are doing compared with others of their age group. These are tests prepared by giving them to a representative group of children of different ages and working out the average score for children in the different age groups. A child will thus be assessed as having a reading age of 7 even though he may be 6 or 8, or even younger or older. This information gives the teacher a clear idea of how well the children are doing compared with others of their age group. Boys and summer-born children tend to score less well than girls and some children make a slow start and catch up later.

Questions for consideration

1   How well and confidently do the children I work with speak and listen? What can I do to help them develop their skill in speaking? How many use standard English naturally?

2   Do the children I work with have opportunities to discuss things in pairs and groups? How good are they at this?

3   What problems do I encounter in hearing reading? What should I do about them?

4   What can I do to encourage more children to enjoy books and reading?

5   What spelling problems do the children encounter? How can I best help them with spelling?

6   Are there children who find it difficult to get started on a piece of writing? What seems to be the best way of helping them?

7   Are there children who find it difficult to punctuate their writing? Can I do anything to help them – perhaps getting them to listen for the way my voice drops at the end of a sentence?

Chapter 9

The core subjects

Mathematics

The National Curriculum for mathematics

The National Curriculum combines with a **Numeracy Strategy**
to set out what is involved in helping children to become numerate.
The Strategy defines numerate pupils as being confident in tackling
problems. They should:

- have a sense of the size of a number and where it fits into the
  number system;
- know basic number facts, such as number bonds, multiplication
  tables, doubles and halves;
- use what they know to figure out an answer mentally;
- calculate accurately, both mentally and with pencil and paper,
  drawing on a range of strategies;
- recognise when it is appropriate to use a calculator and be able
  to do so effectively;
- make sense of number problems, including non-routine problems and recognise the operations needed to solve them;
- explain their methods and their reasoning using correct mathematical terms;
- judge whether their answers are reasonable and have strategies
  for checking them where necessary;
- suggest suitable units for making measurements, and make
  sensible estimates of measurements;
- explain and make predictions from numerical data in a graph,
  chart or table.

Mathematics, like English, is subject to a national strategy that
involves a daily lesson of up to an hour with a clear focus on direct
interactive teaching and interactive oral work with the whole class

and with groups. There is a strong emphasis on mental calculation and the introduction of formal methods of calculating will come later than in the past, with children encouraged to find a variety of ways of calculating before they are introduced to traditional methods.

The lessons, like those for English, are in three parts. The first part involves the whole class in mental calculation, often with children writing their answers on individual whiteboards and holding them up for the teacher to see. Children may also have individual sets of cards with numbers on them that they can hold up to show the teacher their answers. At the early stages the calculations will involve very simple adding and subtracting problems, e.g. I had two sweets and my friend gave me two more; how many do I have? At a later stage the teacher may set them tasks, such as finding out the biggest number that can be made by combining numbers, e.g. 1, 2, 3, 4 and 5, using adding and multiplying, or discovering whether they can work out the four times table by doubling the answers in the two times table. Emphasis will be placed on getting children to explain how they calculated their answers and encouraging them to try different ways of calculating and choosing the most effective.

Part two of the lesson may involve introducing a new topic or consolidating previous work and using and applying knowledge and skill. This may be on a whole-class basis, or working in groups or individually. The teacher may set work for some groups and work with one group him- or herself to teach them something new. Children may be placed in groups by ability with around four groups in the class. This allows the teacher to set work at different levels to cater for children of differing ability. Sometimes this will mean that different groups have different work, with the more able groups being given more challenging work, and sometimes the work will have a common theme with children doing as much as they can. You are likely to be involved with a group, perhaps one that needs extra help to tackle the work of the class.

Early work will involve recognising numerals and there will be much emphasis on counting, both forwards and backwards. Young children given two groups of objects usually start to add them by counting both groups from the beginning. As they progress they learn to count on from the first group. In a similar way they learn to subtract by counting backwards. They also learn to recognise the numbers contained in groups of objects, such as a square (4), a triangle (3) and so on. Children will also learn to measure and weigh objects and will learn about different shapes.

As children get beyond the stage of tasks in single figures, they will learn simple methods of working out sums like 56 + 15. They will be encouraged to work out their own ways of doing this in the first instance and may well discover that one can add the tens to make 60 and the units to make 13. Then 60 and 13 make 73. At later stages more formal methods of calculation will be introduced in this part of the lesson. Children will also learn tables by heart and number bonds to 10 and then 20 and these should be firmly established before formal methods are introduced.

The lesson ends with a plenary session in which the teacher draws together what has been learned, perhaps getting children to say what they now know and can do. This is an opportunity for the teacher to discover whether the children have understood the content of the lesson and to correct any errors in understanding. The teacher may then ask the children to look forward to the next lesson and tell them what will be done then.

Much work, particularly at the early stages, is concentrated on developing concepts. Children need to discover that a group of objects remains the same number whether the objects are grouped close together or spread out. The quantity of water in a container remains the same when it is poured into a differently shaped container. This sounds obvious to an adult, but most young children will say that numbers or quantities have changed until they learn otherwise by experimenting and investigating. This may be something to discuss with younger children when they are playing with water or sand.

A very important concept is that of place value. Children need to learn the value of each number in, say, 364 and understand how important it is to line up the columns in a sum correctly. Children also need to learn the relationship between addition and subtraction and multiplication and division, and discover how they can check their answers by taking away the number that has been added or multiplying the number that has been divided.

A good deal of the work in part two of the lesson will be investigative. It will be planned to help children to recognise and explain patterns and relationships in numbers and shapes and predict and generalise. It might involve working out multiplication tables, halving or doubling numbers or, with older children, calculating the cost of a school journey.

Case study 9.1

Sheila was a newly appointed teaching assistant working with a Year 3 class. She had found mathematics very difficult at school herself, although she had managed to scrape a GCSE pass, and she felt very hesitant about helping children during the numeracy hour. She talked this over with her class teacher, Jonathan, and he suggested that her own problems with mathematics should make her very sympathetic to children who found it difficult. He went on to suggest that she should spend the early part of the lesson observing children to see which of them were not responding and rarely put up their hands to answer a question. She could then target those children in the second part of the lesson and see if she could help them to understand the work that he had been doing with the class.

She felt this would be a possible approach and he suggested that she sat at the front of the class, where she could see all their faces and note those who appeared to be having difficulty.

During part one of the lesson she noted three girls who were not responding and, when the class went on to individual work, she went to the first of the girls and asked her whether she was finding the work too difficult. The girl, Sushila, said she didn't understand what the teacher wanted her to do. Sheila then went to the other two girls and found they made much the same reply, so she gathered them together in a corner of the classroom to go over the work and try to find out where the difficulty was. They had been asked to add different length measures and she found that they had a very limited concept of measurement. She set them to work to measure things in the classroom and she invented problems where measurements needed to be added together. They worked at this and eventually found that they could do it.

Studies of the effect of the Numeracy Strategy have found that boys in all age groups were frequently scoring higher than girls. Indian and Chinese pupils had higher scores than white pupils in all age groups and Black Afro-Caribbean children often had lower scores.

The use of calculators

Children will be introduced to calculators at some stage. The timing of this varies a good deal from school to school. Calculators make it possible for children to do calculations that they might otherwise find too difficult. Calculators also make it possible to use real-life problems, where the numbers would otherwise be difficult for the children to handle. They are also valuable in getting children to discover patterns and rules for dealing with numbers. They should not be used as a substitute for mental calculation and most schools will probably delay their introduction until children are fairly proficient calculators.

Key Stage 1: the infant school

During Key Stage 1 most children should learn to do the following:

*   Count reliably at least 20 objects and gradually extend their counting to 100 and beyond.
*   Know by heart all pairs of numbers with a total of 10 and use these to derive facts with totals of up to 20. Know the two and ten times tables and be able to work out the corresponding division facts. Be able to add and subtract 10 from any given two-digit number. Carry out simple calculations using the symbols for addition, subtraction, multiplication and division.
*   Be able to solve problems involving numbers presented in a variety of forms, making appropriate decisions about which strategies to use.
*   Understand that addition can be done in any order and that subtraction is the inverse of addition and conversely addition is the inverse of subtraction. Understand subtraction as both 'difference' and 'take away'. Understand multiplication as repeated addition and begin to understand division as repeated subtraction.
*   Recognise triangles, quadrilaterals, prisms and pyramids, right angles, perpendicular and parallel lines and described properties of shapes. Estimate and measure the size of objects and weigh objects and calculate capacity.

Key Stage 2: the junior school

At Key Stage 2 most children should learn to do the following:

- Count on and back in tens or hundreds from any two- or three-digit number, extending this to negative numbers when counting back.
- Recognise and describe number patterns, such as multiples of 2, 5 or 10, recognise prime numbers to 20 and square numbers up to 10 × 10. Find factors for two-digit numbers.
- Understand fractions such as one-third or five-eighths and be able to find fractions of shapes and quantities. Be able to find common denominators. Recognise equivalence of decimals and fractions of halves, quarters, tenths and hundredths. Understand the meaning of percentage.
- Understand and use decimal notation for tenths and hundredths in amounts of money, length etc.
- Recall all addition and subtraction facts for each number to 20. Handle additions and subtractions of three- and four-digit numbers. Recall multiplication facts to 10 × 10 and use them to derive the corresponding division facts. Double and halve two-digit numbers. Multiply and divide at first in the range 1–100 and then larger numbers.
- Recognise the need for standard units of measurement. Select and use appropriate calculation skills to solve geometrical problems.

Case study 9.2

Jack was a teaching assistant in a Year 2 class in which children were starting to learn the two and ten times tables. The class teacher talked about doubling and counting in tens and started by getting the children to count in twos to a hundred, going round the class so that each child had to answer in turn. They could do this fairly well with only one or two children stumbling when it was their turn. She then got them to count in tens and most of them could do this too. She next gave them some written work to do and asked Jack to work with a small group of children who had found the initial work too difficult.

Jack started by explaining that multiplying by two was called doubling a number and he talked about a situation in which they needed twice as many plates on the table as a family of four usually had because they had four guests. They found this quite easy and went on to practise doubling the numbers to 10 and then to 20.

He then described a situation where two children had a bar of ten pieces of chocolate and asked how many each would get when they divided it between them. They managed this easily and went on to halve other numbers. They then practised counting in twos to 40 and on to a 100. Next he asked them whether they could work out what double 20 would be. After a slow start they showed they were able to do this and he went on to ask them what double 30 would be and then double 40. They soon grasped the relationship of these tasks to doubling units and could double numbers up to 200.

Assessment and evaluation

As in English, children are regularly assessed by their teacher and are tested nationally at 7 and 11 years of age. Both assessments are expressed in terms of levels of attainment. Levels are numbered 1 to 5 as in English and the average 7-year-old is expected to reach level 2 and the average 11-year-old, level 4. Parents should be informed about the level their child has reached.

At level 1, pupils use mathematics as parts of classroom activities and count, order, add and subtract numbers when solving problems involving up to ten objects. They learn about two- and three-dimensional shapes and use everyday language to describe properties and positions. They measure objects and sort and classify them according to different criteria.

At level 2, pupils count more reliably and use mental recall of addition and subtraction facts to 10. They begin to understand the place value of each digit in a number up to 100. They choose the appropriate operation when solving addition and subtraction problems and know that subtraction is the inverse of addition. They recognise odd and even numbers and use mental calculation to solve number problems involving money and measures. They use mathematical names for common two- and three-dimensional shapes and understand angles as a measurement of turn and recognise right angles. They begin to use standard units of measurement. They sort and classify objects using more than one criterion and record results in simple lists, tables and block graphs.

At level 3, pupils are beginning to be able to explain their thinking about mathematical problems and check their results. They show understanding of place value in numbers up to 1,000 and begin to use decimal notation. They add and subtract numbers with two digits mentally and numbers with three digits using written methods. They use mental recall of the two, three, four, five and ten times tables and derive the associated division facts. They solve whole-number problems involving multiplication and division, including those with remainders. They use simple fractions. They classify two- and three-dimensional shapes, and use non-standard and standard metric units to measure length and weight. They extract and interpret information presented in simple tables and lists, and construct bar charts and pictograms to communicate information they have gathered.

At level 4, pupils are developing their own strategies for solving problems and search for a solution by trying out ideas of their own. They use their knowledge of place value to multiply and divide whole numbers by ten and use efficient written methods of addition and subtraction and short multiplication and division. They add and subtract decimals to two places and check the reasonableness of their answers by reference to their knowledge of the context or to the size of the numbers. They make three-dimensional mathematical models. They choose and use appropriate units and measuring instruments. They construct and interpret simple line graphs.

At level 5, pupils are beginning to show understanding of situations by describing them mathematically using symbols, words and diagrams. They can explain their reasoning. They have a good understanding of place value and can multiply and divide whole numbers and decimals by 10, 100 and 1,000. They are able to use negative numbers. They use addition, subtraction, multiplication and division with decimals to two places, and can work with fractions and percentages. They can measure and draw angles to the nearest degree and know the rough metric equivalents of imperial measures still in use. They make sensible estimates in relation to everyday situations. They can interpret graphs and diagrams and pie charts and have some understanding of probability.

Mathematics across the curriculum

Schools are expected to look at the way in which other subjects of the curriculum use mathematics and where possible to link these to the mathematics programme. For example, there will be a good deal of measuring in technology and in science and, since in most cases the same teacher will be dealing with these subjects as well as mathematics, the links will be easy to make. Cooking in technology will involve weighing and measuring. With older children there will be work in geography involving maps and the use of different scales. Children will learn about different countries and may need to get an idea of the distances they are from Britain. In history there will be some work with dates and children will need to learn how long ago some things happened.

Numeracy skills

Children will often turn to you for help in working out what to do in number. As with spelling, it is usually a good idea to ask children what they think they should do before making suggestions yourself. In helping, suggest a first step and ask the child what s/he thinks should be done next, leading the child towards a solution by further questions. At each stage suggest ways of remembering the procedure if this is appropriate.

You may also be involved in helping children with weighing or measuring. With young children this should always be a practical activity with plenty of opportunity to weigh and measure and perhaps estimate the weight or measurement of something and check to see what it really is.

Suggestions for learning and practising tables

There are many ways of helping children to learn number bonds and tables and practise them until they are automatic knowledge. At the early stages you will need to do this practically, with children building pairs of numbers that make 10 from counters or coins or building a multiplication table. When they get more competent, it is a good time to play a board game with a small group, such as Snakes and Ladders or Ludo, with the children having to solve a number problem before they can make each move. Another ploy is to make a card or worksheet for each member of a group with some number bonds or simple multiplication sums but without answers. The children can then have a race to see who can finish first and get them all right.

Questions for consideration

1   What concepts are the children in the class I work with in the process of learning? What can I do to help their understanding?

2   What knowledge are they in the process of acquiring? How can I make acquiring it interesting for them?

3   What skills should they be developing? How can I help them?

4   How can I provide practise of number bonds and table facts?

5   How can I best help children to develop skill in measuring and weighing?

6   How well do the children I am working with understand place value?

Chapter 10

The core subjects

Science

Science is the third core subject of the National Curriculum. At the primary stage of education it is about stimulating children's curiosity about the world around them and exploring the environment, asking questions, speculating about the answers and seeking ways to find out whether the speculations are true. Children approach science with ideas of their own about why things are the way they are and these theories are often incompatible with the ideas teachers want them to learn. It is therefore important that there is a good deal of discussion about the observations children make in their science lessons so that teachers can be aware of children's misconceptions and lead them to more accurate theories. Some of these discussions will be with you and you will gain ideas about what children are thinking about scientific issues, which will be of interest to your teacher.

Teaching science at the primary stage is also about developing attitudes. Valuable attitudes at this stage are curiosity, open-mindedness and perseverance, coupled with the ability to be self-critical and self-disciplined and to cooperate with other people. There are also important skills to develop. Children need to learn to investigate by observing, drawing conclusions from their observations and looking for patterns that enable them to suggest reasons for what they observe. They then need to plan investigations to see if their conclusions were correct, interpret their findings and record and report what they have found out. Much of this exploration will be of the local environment. The teacher's role in their investigation, working with you, will be to provide the opportunity for studying and interacting with the environment, designing tasks that encourage discussion in small groups leading to whole-class discussions, providing access to other information and helping children to find ways of expressing what they have found out.

You will probably be involved in working with a group investigating something, possibly in the environment, and helping them as they explore the natural and man-made world around them, then helping them to find ways of testing out their ideas and developing them to explain what they find. In this way they may develop skill in forming and testing ideas.

Key Stage 1: the infant school

At Key Stage 1, children are encouraged to ask questions about everyday experience, looking at how and why things are as they are and wondering what would happen if something were changed. They are encouraged to use first-hand experience and simple information sources to find answers to their questions. They learn to make observations and communicate their findings, considering evidence, trying to explain it and comparing what actually happened with what they thought would happen.

Life processes

They learn about life processes and living things, and how to understand the difference between things that are living, things that were once living but are now dead and things that have never been alive. They learn that animals, including human beings, move, feed, grow, use their senses and reproduce, relating this to animals found in the local environment and to themselves. They learn about the bodies of people and animals and that living creatures need food and water to stay alive. They also learn about the value of taking exercise and eating the right kinds of food. Children should be taught that plants need light and water to grow and that they reproduce through seed.

Materials

At Key Stage 1, children also learn about materials, using their senses to explore and recognise the similarities and differences between different materials and sort objects into groups on the basis of simple properties such as hardness, softness, roughness, shininess, ability to float, and so on. They learn about the uses of different materials and explore the way some materials can be changed by heating or cooling.

Physical processes

Physical processes, such as electricity, are studied and children learn about simple circuits, using batteries, wires and bulbs, and the role of switches. They learn about forces and motion. They also learn about making and detecting sound.

Key Stage 2: the junior school

At this stage, children learn about a wider range of living things, materials and phenomena, applying their knowledge of scientific ideas in various ways. They carry out more systematic investigations working on their own and with others and use a range of reference sources in their work. They learn to ask questions that can be investigated scientifically and consider what sources of information they can use. They learn how to make a fair test by changing one factor and observing or measuring the effect while keeping the other factors the same. They make systematic observations and measurements and use a range of ways to communicate their findings.

Life processes

Children learn more about life processes common to humans and other animals, such as nutrition, movement, growth and reproduction, and the life processes in plants. They learn about circulation, body muscles and bones and the main stages of the human life cycle. They also learn about the effects of tobacco, alcohol and other drugs on health. They learn about plant reproduction and the parts of the flower. They study the relationship between plants and animals and their habitat and learn about food chains.

Case study 10.1

Ginny worked with Mary, the teacher of a Year 5 class, and in the second half of the Spring Term the class spent time on plant growth and reproduction. The school had a large playing field with many trees and other plants growing round its edges. The class was divided into groups, each with a particular task to do outside in the playing field. Ginny had a group of six children and the teacher asked her to get them to study the trees. Fortunately, she knew about this a few days in advance, so she was able to look round and see what trees there were and find books about trees from which the children could find out more. There was a good variety – oak, ash, hornbeam, beech, sycamore, silver birch, lime and horse chestnut.

They walked round the field looking at each of the trees in turn and discussing what made each one different. Ginny suggested that each child pick a leaf from each tree to make a collection of leaves. Some of the trees had branches too high for the children to reach but they found leaves for those trees lying on the ground and everyone managed to get a full collection.

When they got back to the classroom, Ginny showed them how to make prints of the leaves by covering the backs with paint and pressing them down on to paper. Each child made eight prints, one for each tree, and they then helped each other to remember which tree each leaf came from. When the prints were dry they labelled them.

Ginny then got them to look at some books on trees she had brought from the library to see what they could find out about each tree, in preparation for telling the rest of the class what they had done. They found out a number of interesting things, such as what the wood of each tree was used for and the age some of the trees lived to. They also found out about the way each tree flowered and the seed that came from the flowers. The talk to the class went well and the next day they wrote about what they discovered about each tree and Ginny mounted their prints and the written work to make a classroom display.

Materials

In learning about materials children look at the properties of everyday objects – their hardness, strength, flexibility and magnetic behaviour – and relate these properties to everyday uses of the materials. They study rocks and soil and learn to describe their characteristics, such as appearance, texture and permeability. They learn to recognise differences between solids, liquids and gases. Experiments enable children to describe changes when materials are mixed, heated or cooled, and they learn about changes that happen when materials are dissolved, melted, boiled, condensed, frozen or evaporated. They learn that some changes are reversible and others are not.

Physical processes

Children develop further the work they did at Key Stage 1 on electricity and learn to construct circuits, incorporating a power supply and a range of switches, and to make drawings and diagrams of these using conventional symbols.

They learn about magnetism and gravity and about friction, including air resistance and how to measure forces and the direction in which they act. They learn about light, reflections, shadows, vibrations and sound. They study the sun, earth and moon and how the position of the sun appears to change during the day and how shadows change as this happens.

In the course of this work children learn to use appropriate scientific language and terms to communicate ideas and explain the behaviour of living things, materials, phenomena and processes.

Assessment and evaluation

Children are assessed annually by their teachers for their progress in science and are tested nationally at age 11. Your observations will be helpful to the teacher in making these assessments. As in English and mathematics, the science results are given in levels and you need to know about these. The results of the SATs and the teacher assessment will be communicated to parents in each child's annual report. The average child should achieve level 2 at the end of Key Stage 1 and level 4 at the end of Key Stage 2.

At level 1, children should be able to describe or respond appropriately to the features of objects, living things and events they observe and communicate their observations by talking about them, making drawings or completing simple charts. They should recognise and name parts of the body and parts of plants and a range of common animals. They should know about a range of properties of materials, such as texture and appearance, and communicate observations of changes in light, sound or movement that result from actions such as switching on a simple electrical circuit or pushing and pulling objects.

At level 2, children should begin to make suggestions about how to collect information in order to find things out and use simple texts to find information and make observations related to the task they are undertaking. They should observe and compare objects, living things and events and are beginning to use scientific language and record their findings. They should be able to use their knowledge about living things to describe what animals and plants need in order to survive (such as a supply of food, water, air, light) and can sort living things into groups according to their features and know that living things grow and reproduce. They should be able to identify a range of common materials and know some of their properties and use these to sort them into groups using everyday terms such as shininess, hardness and smoothness. They should be able to describe ways in which some materials are changed by heating or cooling or by processes such as bending or stretching. They should know about a range of physical phenomena and compare lights by brightness or colour and sounds by loudness or pitch and compare the movement of different objects in terms of speed or direction.

At level 3, children should be able to put forward their own ideas about how to find the answer to a question and recognise the need to collect information in order to answer questions, making relevant observations and measuring quantities, such as length, weight or volume. They should be able to carry out a fair test and recognise why it is fair, recording their observations in a variety of ways and communicating using scientific language. They should be able to describe differences between living and non-living things and provide explanations for changes in living things, such as the effect of diet on health, and the effects of lack of light or water on plant growth. They should be able to explain why some materials are suitable for particular purposes and recognise that some changes in materials can be reversed and others cannot. They should be able to use their knowledge of physical phenomena to explain such things as a bulb failing to light because of a break in the electrical circuit.

At level 4, children should recognise that scientific ideas are based on evidence and be able to select an appropriate approach to find the answer to a question (for example, using a fair test). They should be able to make predictions and select equipment and make observations to see if their predictions are correct. They should record their observations and findings using tables and bar charts and begin to plot simple graphs, using them to point out patterns in their findings and communicate using scientific language. They should use scientific names for the organs of the body systems and know their position, and they should know the names of the parts of plants. They should learn about the food chains of plants and animals. They should be able to describe differences between the properties of materials and explain how these differences are used to classify substances such as solids, liquids and gases. They should also be able to describe some of the methods used to separate simple mixtures and use scientific language to describe changes. They should demonstrate knowledge and understanding of physical processes and make generalisations about physical phenomena, such as gravitation, magnetism and friction. They should be able to describe and explain physical phenomena (e.g. how a particular device may be connected to work in an electrical circuit or how the apparent position of the sun changes in the course of a day).

Children at level 5 should be able to identify an appropriate approach to find the answer to a scientific question and make predictions based on their scientific knowledge and understanding and select apparatus appropriately. They should be able to make observations, comparisons and measurements with precision appropriate to the task and record observations and measurements systematically. They should then use appropriate scientific language to communicate their findings. They should demonstrate an increasing knowledge of life processes and living things, and describe the functions of the main organs of the human body and of plants, and know the main stages of the life cycles of humans, animals and flowering plants, recognising the importance of habitat. They should demonstrate knowledge of materials and their properties. They should be able to use ideas to explain how to make a range of changes (e.g. altering the current in a circuit, altering the pitch or loudness of a sound) and use simple models to explain effects that are caused by the movement of the earth.

A survey by the Office for Standards in Education (Ofsted) in 1996–7 found that four-fifths of children in the infant school (Key Stage 1) achieved or exceeded the expected National Curriculum level in science and more than two-thirds did so at the junior school level (Key Stage 2). Teachers' knowledge of this subject was now satisfactory in 90 per cent of schools and good in well over a third.

Your class teacher will have ideas about ways in which children can become involved in scientific work and will welcome any ideas you may have about how the work can be developed. Young children are naturally curious and this can be encouraged by asking them to speculate about why things happen and what would happen if the situation were somewhat different. There may be opportunities for identifying plants and trees in the environment.

Some suggestions for investigation

Work with a group of children collecting different seeds, plant them and watch them grow. Get children to measure the plants day by day to see how much they grow in a week or a fortnight and draw graphs of this. Try setting up experiments with pairs of plants, placing one on a sunny windowsill and another in a shady corner, or watering one more than another and observing the effect on growth. Children can make books or a display of drawings or paintings of plants found and this encourages detailed observation of parts of the plant and how they fit together.

Observing birds is another activity that children can enjoy. Here again they can be encouraged to observe the colouring and shape of birds that come to a bird table or to a lawn and look them up in a bird book to find out what they are and their characteristics. Children can try to discover the food that birds eat apart from what is given them by humans.

You can observe shadows with children. How do they change during the course of a day? You could help the children make a simple sundial and use it to tell the time by using the shadow. You can also observe the weather together, looking at the sorts of clouds in the sky and seeing if there are patterns in the cloud formation, sunsets and the weather following. Is the old rhyme about red sky at night true? A child might enjoy keeping a diary of the weather each day and illustrating it.

Questions for consideration

1 What is there in the school environment that could be used in the study of science?
2 What sorts of ideas have the children I work with about everyday science, such as how electrical equipment works?
3 What sorts of ideas have they about human and animal bodies?

4   How do they think plants reproduce?
5   Are the children I work with developing ideas for testing out their own theories? How can I best help this?
6   Are the children developing observation skills and the ability to draw valid conclusions from their observations?

Chapter 11

The foundation subjects

The National Curriculum identifies eight foundation subjects and the curriculum also includes RE, which is not at present part of the National Curriculum but is still a compulsory subject. You need to have some idea about all of these because you will be expected to help children with all their studies.

Art and design

The National Curriculum makes the following statement about art and design:

> Art and design stimulates creativity and imagination. It provides visual, tactile and sensory experiences and a unique way of understanding and responding to the world. Pupils use colour, form, texture, pattern and different materials and processes to communicate what they see, feel and think. Through art and design activities, they learn to make informed value judgements and aesthetic and practical decisions, becoming actively involved in shaping environments. They study the work of artists and designers and learn to enjoy the visual arts.

Children go through a succession of stages in learning to draw. A very young child given drawing materials will scribble. Gradually, the scribbles are replaced by more carefully drawn shapes, which the child may label as people or objects. The shapes become the symbols we see in young children's drawings for houses, trees and people. The sky is drawn at the top of the paper and the earth at the bottom. Interest in detail gradually grows until the child is drawing more from observation than using symbolic shapes.

Key Stage 1: the infant school

Children learn to record from first-hand observation and investigate the possibilities of different materials and processes, using different tools and techniques. They learn to evaluate their own work and that of others. They learn about colour, pattern and texture, line and tone, shape, form and space. They look at the work of artists and craftspeople from different times and cultures. They explore a range of starting points for practical work and sometimes work collaboratively with others. They explore painting, collage, print-making, textiles, sculpture and ICT.

Key Stage 2: the junior school

At this stage children increase their skills and control of materials and tools. They record from experience and imagination, using first-hand observation. They collect visual information and may use a sketchbook. They investigate and combine visual and tactile qualities of materials and use a variety of methods and approaches to communicate observations, ideas and feelings and to design and make images and artefacts. They evaluate their own work and that of others and consider how a piece of work might be improved. They study the work of artists and craftspeople from different periods and cultures. They explore a range of starting points for work, such as their own experiences, images, stories, drama, music, natural and man-made objects and the work of artists and crafts-people. They explore different techniques and materials.

Design and technology

Design and technology is a comparatively new subject in the school curriculum at the primary stage. The National Curriculum states:

> Design and technology prepares pupils to participate in tomorrow's rapidly changing technologies. They learn to think creatively to improve the quality of life. The subject calls for pupils to become autonomous and creative problem-solvers, as individuals and as members of a team. They must look for needs and opportunities and respond to them by developing a range of ideas and making products and systems. They combine practical skills with an understanding of aesthetics, social and

environmental issues, function and industrial practices. As they do so, they reflect on and evaluate present and past design and technology, its uses and effects. Through design and technology, all pupils can become discriminating and informed users of products and become innovators.

Key Stage 1: the infant school

At this stage children learn to develop ideas, communicating them in a variety of ways, including drawing and making models. They learn to work with tools and different materials, such as wood, fabric, cardboard and food of various kinds, to make quality products, measuring and marking out, cutting and shaping materials and treating them in different ways for various purposes. They learn different ways of joining materials and finishing their work. They learn to do simple cooking as well as make artefacts. They learn to evaluate what they have made, talking about what they like and dislike about it and what they could have done differently. They learn about qualities of materials and how mechanisms, such as wheels, axles and joints that allow movement, can be used in various ways. They also learn to evaluate existing products, talking about how they work and whether they do what they are supposed to do. They learn about the need for safe working practices.

Key Stage 2: the junior school

During Key Stage 2, children work both alone and as part of a team on designing and making activities. They learn to think about the people who might use what they make and what their products could be used for. They develop and explain ideas about what their design should achieve. They learn to select appropriate tools and materials for the work they plan and measure, mark out, cut and shape materials and assemble and join them to make a finished product, using a range of equipment, sometimes including ICT. They learn to reflect on their work and test out the quality of what they have made to see how well it fits its purpose. They gradually become more knowledgeable about the properties of the various materials they are using. They learn about how different mechanisms can be used to make things move in different ways using different equipment, including ICT. They learn how electrical circuits work using simple switches and this can link up with work in science. They will also investigate and evaluate a range of familiar products. They will develop further the work on food already started at Key Stage 1.

Geography

The National Curriculum for geography states:

> Geography provokes and answers questions about the natural and human worlds, using different types of enquiry to view them from different perspectives. It develops knowledge of places and environments throughout the world, an understanding of maps, and a range of investigative and problem-solving skills both inside and outside the classroom. As such, it prepares pupils for adult life and employment. Geography is a focus within the curriculum for understanding and resolving issues about the environment and sustainable development. It is also an important link between the natural and social sciences. As pupils study geography, they encounter different societies and cultures. This helps them realise how nations rely on each other. It can inspire them to think about their own place in the world, their values, and their rights and responsibilities to other people and the environment.

Geography is about the relationship between the earth and the people who live on it. Children study different environments, the way people live in them and the use they make of the earth's resources. They learn to consider what a place is like and how it differs from the environments they know. They learn about climate, its causes and its effects on the environment. They learn to use and interpret maps, to understand map symbols and conventions and to use a compass. They learn about physical geography and study the way rocks are transformed by weathering and erosion.

A very important part of geography is fieldwork. At all stages children should have the opportunity to study different environments first-hand.

Key Stage 1: the infant school

At this stage children consider what it is like to live in a particular place and start to use geographical vocabulary, such as hill, river, motorway, near, far, north, south, east and west. They learn how to use globes, maps and plans with different scales and make picture maps and plans. They begin to be able to identify where places are on a map and what they are like in terms of landscape, climate and how they compare with other places, for example how their local area compares with other places in the United Kingdom. They make observations about the local environment, including the weather, and start to consider how the environment may be improved and sustained.

Key Stage 2: the junior school

At this stage children should start to develop geographical skills and use appropriate geographical vocabulary, such as temperature, transport and industry. They learn to use fieldwork techniques, such as labelled field sketches, and use globes, maps and plans with a range of scales, as well as secondary sources of information, such as aerial photographs. They learn to draw plans and maps with different scales. They increase their knowledge and understanding of places and are able to identify what places are like in terms of weather, local resources and occupations. They learn about why places are like they are and how and why places change and how places fit into larger regions or countries. They consider how people can improve the environment or damage it.

During this Key Stage children study a locality in the United Kingdom and one in a country that is less economically developed. They study water and its effects on landscapes and people, how settlements differ and change and an environmental issue. Studies should include fieldwork outside the classroom.

History

The National Curriculum (1999) makes the following statement about the aims of teaching history:

> History fires pupil's curiosity about the past in Britain and the wider world. Pupils consider how the past influences the present, what past societies were like, how these societies organ-ised their politics, and what beliefs and cultures influenced people's actions. As they do this, pupils develop a chronolog-ical framework for their knowledge of significant events and

people. They see the diversity of human experience, and understand more about themselves as individuals and members of society. What they learn can influence their decisions about personal choices, attitudes and values.

An important part of learning in history is the consideration of historical evidence. Evidence may be oral, as when children talk with their parents and grandparents to find out what life was like when they were children, or it may involve maps, pictures and photographs, parish records, artefacts or writing. They need to learn to weigh up evidence and consider its significance. Where was it found? What does it tell us about the people who created it?

Over the years of primary education, children develop their ideas or concepts about the past. Initially, their understanding of words such as kingdom, society, war, defence, change, trade, ceremony, civilisation, development, and so on will be very different from that of an adult, and gradually they come to understand how the past differs from the present and gain ideas about the passage of time. Discussion is important in this work so that the teacher can assess the degree of understanding children are achieving. They also need to learn to distinguish between fact and opinion.

Work in history is likely to involve some visits to historical sites or museums to see things first-hand. A visit to an iron-age site, for example, might involve children thinking how they would have built shelters for themselves if they had lived then, what they would have eaten, where they might have found water, and how they would have made tools and organised themselves. There should also be opportunities for children to look at historical artefacts, perhaps in a museum, and draw conclusions from them.

Key stage I: the infant school

At this stage children learn about significant men, women and children, and events from the recent and more distant past, and hear stories that help them to understand how the past is different from the present. They learn the language needed for talking about the past, such as 'a long time ago', and begin to place events in chronological order and identify the differences between ways of life in the past and life in the present day. They learn about sources of information about the past, such as stories, eyewitness accounts, pictures and photographs, artefacts, historic buildings, visits to museums and ICT-based resources. They learn about the way of life of people in the recent and more distant past and the lives of significant men and women and children, such as artists, engineers, musicians, explorers, inventors, pioneers, rulers, saints and scientists. They also learn about significant events in the history of Britain.

Key stage 2: the junior school

At this stage children learn about change and continuity in their own area and in Britain and other parts of the world. They look at history in a variety of ways, for example from political, economic, techno-logical and scientific, social, religious, cultural or aesthetic perspec-tives, using a variety of sources of information and using dates and historical vocabulary to describe events, people and developments.

They learn to use dates to place events in time and learn about the characteristics of different societies in the past in Britain and the wider world and begin to understand the reasons for, and the results of, historical events and changes in the periods studied. They learn that the past can be represented and interpreted in different ways and the reasons for this. They learn to use a variety of resources for studying the past and communicate their learning and under-standing in a variety of ways.

Work at this stage should include a study of an aspect of the local area, a study of the Romans, Anglo-Saxons and Vikings in Britain, a study of Britain and the wider world in Tudor times and either a study of the Victorians or of Britain since 1930. There should also be a study of ancient Greece and a world history study.

Information and communication technology (ICT)

The National Curriculum makes the following statement about ICT:

> Information and communication technology (ICT) prepares pupils to participate in a rapidly changing world in which work and other activities are increasingly transformed by access to varied and developing technology. Pupils use ICT tools to find, explore, analyse, exchange and present information responsibly, creatively and with discrimination. They learn how to employ ICT to enable rapid access to ideas and experiences from a

wide range of people, communities and cultures. Increased capability in the use of ICT promotes initiative and independent learning, with pupils being able to make informed judgements about when and where to use ICT to best effect, and to consider its implications for home and work both now and in the future.

This subject plays an increasing part in children's education and is important in preparing them for the adult world. They learn to use ICT to find, explore, analyse, exchange and present information creatively and with discrimination.

Key Stage 1: the infant school

At this stage children learn to gather information from various sources and enter and store it in a variety of forms and retrieve it when needed. They learn to use text, tables, images and sound to develop their ideas and how to select from, and add to, information and have opportunities to try things out. They learn to present information effectively in different forms. They explore a variety of uses of ICT, using it to support their work in other subjects.

Key Stage 2: the junior school

Children at this stage talk about the information they need and how they can find and use it. They learn how to interpret information and develop ideas by bringing together text, tables, images and sound and making multimedia presentations. They learn how to share and exchange information and use email and how to be sensitive to audience and readership. They learn how to make and use spreadsheets and databases. They use ICT as part of their learning in various areas of the curriculum.

Music

The National Curriculum makes the following statement about music:

Music is a powerful, unique form of communication that can change the way pupils feel, think and act. It brings together intellect and feeling and enables personal expression, reflection and emotional development. As an integral part of culture, past and present, it helps pupils understand themselves and relate to others, forging important links between the home, school and the wider world. The teaching of music develops pupils' ability to listen and appreciate a wide variety of music and to make judgements about musical quality. It encourages active involvement in different forms of amateur music making, both individual and communal, developing a sense of group identity and togetherness. It also increases self-discipline and creativity, aesthetic sensitivity and fulfilment.

Key Stage 1: the infant school

At this stage children use their voices to sing and have the opportunity to play tuned and untuned instruments, individually and in a group, and to listen to different kinds of music. They learn to create musical patterns and explore, choose and organise sounds and musical ideas. They learn to express their ideas about the way music makes them feel, using movement, dance and language. They learn to listen with concentration and recall sounds and find different ways of making sounds. They undertake a range of musical activities that involve performing, composing and appraising.

Key Stage 2: the junior school

At this stage listening, applying knowledge and understanding are developed through the interrelated skills of performing, composing and appraising. Pupils sing songs in unison and in two parts, with clear diction and musical expression. They play tuned and untuned instruments with control and accuracy and present performances. They develop skill in composing and learn how the musical elements of pitch, duration, tempo, timbre, texture and silence can be organised within musical structures to communicate different moods and ideas. They listen to a range of music from different periods and cultures.

Personal, social and health education (PSHE)

The National Curriculum describes the purposes of PSHE as follows:

Personal, social and health education (PSHE) and citizenship help to give pupils the knowledge, skills and understanding they need to lead confident, healthy, independent lives and to become informed, active, responsible citizens. Pupils are encouraged to take part in a wide range of activities and experiences across and beyond the curriculum, contributing fully to the life of their school and communities. In doing so they learn to recognise their own worth, work well with others and become increasingly responsible for their own learning. They reflect on their experiences and understand how they are developing personally and socially, tackling many of the spiritual, moral, social and cultural issues that are part of growing up. They also find out about the main political and social institutions that affect their lives and about their responsibilities, rights and duties as individuals and members of communities. They learn to understand and respect our common humanity, diversity and differences so that they can go on to form the effective, fulfilling relationships that are an essential part of life and learning.

Key Stage 1: the infant school

At this stage children learn about themselves as members of the school and local communities, building on their own experiences and on the work done at the pre-school stage. They learn about how to keep themselves healthy and safe and about good behaviour. They learn to take some responsibility for themselves and their environment. They begin to learn about their own and other people's feelings and become aware of the views, needs and rights of other children and older people. They learn social skills, such as how to share, take turns, play, help others, resolve simple arguments and resist bullying. They begin to take an active part in the life of their school and its neighbourhood.

Key Stage 2: the junior school

At this stage children continue to learn about themselves as growing and changing individuals with their own experiences and ideas, and as members of their school and community. As they grow they become more mature, independent and self-confident. They learn about the wider world and the interdependence of communities within it. They develop their sense of social justice and moral responsibility and begin to understand that their own choices and behaviour can affect local, national or global issues and political and social institutions. They learn how to take part more fully in school and community activities. They learn how to make more confident and informed choices about their health and environment, how to take more responsibility, individually and as a group, for their own learning and how to resist bullying.

Physical education (PE)

The National Curriculum for PE makes the following statement:

> Physical education develops pupils' physical competence and confidence, and their ability to use these to perform in a range of activities. It promotes physical skilfulness, physical development and a knowledge of the body in action. Physical education provides opportunities for pupils to be creative, competitive and to face up to different challenges as individuals and in groups and teams. It promotes positive attitudes towards active and healthy lifestyles.

Key Stage 1: the infant school

At this stage children build on their natural enthusiasm for movement and explore basic movement skills with increasing control and coordination, choosing and applying skills to develop sequences of actions. They learn to describe what they have done and observe, describe and copy what others have done. They learn how important it is to be active for good health and they enjoy dance, games and gymnastics. They learn how to use movement imaginatively in dance, responding to stimuli, including music, and create and perform simple movement patterns. They should be taught to play with a ball and other equipment and play simple games. In gymnastics they should develop their range of skills and actions, such as balancing, taking off and landing, turning and rolling, and should create movement sequences. In swimming they should learn to move in water, float and move with and without swimming aids and start to use arm and leg actions and basic swimming strokes.

Key Stage 2: the junior school

During Key Stage 2 children enjoy being active and learn to use their creativity and imagination in physical activity. They consolidate their existing skills, learn new ones and increase their control. They learn to plan activities in small groups and pairs and evaluate their performance and that of others and suggest ways of improving it. They should learn about fitness and health. All children should learn dance, games and gymnastics and two activities from swimming and water safety, athletic activities and outdoor and adventurous activities. In dance they learn to create and perform dances using a range of movement patterns. They learn to play a number of games and in gymnastics they learn to create and perform movement sequences on the floor and using apparatus. In swimming they learn to swim unaided using a range of recognised stokes. Athletics involves running, jumping and throwing in combination, and outdoor education involves taking part in outdoor activity challenges, in familiar and unfamiliar environments.

Religious education (RE)

RE is rather different from the other subjects in that it is not part of the National Curriculum but is taught according to a locally provided Agreed Syllabus, except in church-aided schools, where it is taught according to the scheme set out by the particular denomination. It is nevertheless a compulsory part of the school curriculum. Each LEA has to set up a Standing Advisory Council for Religious Education (**SACRE**), which is a group of representatives of the different faiths in the area and representative teachers and is responsible for the Agreed Syllabus for their area. This means that there may be some local differences in what is taught, though there is likely to be a good deal of agreement between the different syllabuses.

The 1944 Education Act, which laid down the arrangements for RE, requires that an Agreed Syllabus should not reflect any particular religious denomination and a more recent ruling stresses that RE must not be designed to convert pupils to a particular belief. The Education Act of 1996 states that the Agreed Syllabus should reflect the fact that the religious traditions of Great Britain are in the main Christian, while taking account of the teaching of other religions represented in the country.

RE should aim to give children knowledge of Christianity and the other principal religions represented in Britain and help to develop their awareness of the fundamental questions of life and the way religious teachings relate to them. It is also concerned with developing respect and a positive attitude towards people of different faiths and cultures.

Key Stage 1: the infant school

Provision for children at this stage in most syllabuses is likely to include stories from different religious traditions and stories about religious leaders. There will probably be some work on exploring the difference between right and wrong. Children should have the

---

Project work

Many primary school teachers do some work that covers a whole range of subjects. A class in a village school might, for instance, make a study of their village. This would involve some geography in studying and making maps to show where the village is situated and the roads round about and in looking at the occupations of the people in the village. Children might make a model of the village, which would involve mathematics and technology. History could be involved in studying the houses, the church and other buildings in the village. The school logbooks might yield interesting evidence. Children might also talk to parents and grandparents about times past. They might make drawings and paintings of parts of the village as part of their art work. Science might be involved in the study of flowers and trees in the vicinity. RE might involve learning more about the church and what went on there. English would be involved in most of the work as children wrote up what they had found out. ICT might be involved in recording the findings and there might be interesting and relevant information on the internet. The work could be gathered together to make an exhibition about the village, which parents and grandparents could be invited to see.

opportunity to develop a sense of their own identity as individuals and members of communities and different faiths. They may learn about different places of worship and celebrations and festivals in different religions. In church-aided schools, too, this kind of ground will probably be covered, as well as the particular beliefs and practices of their own church and faith.

Key Stage 2: the junior school

At this stage children are likely to develop further their knowledge of different religions and consider stories and practices that focus on values, relationships and religious teaching and the relevance of these to their own lives. They will study the life and teaching of Jesus and the way in which key events in his life are celebrated. They will probably study other religions in some detail and perhaps visit places of worship.

The role of the teaching assistant

In all these subjects you will be acting in a supportive role, which is why you need to know something about them. In most subjects you will be concerned with helping children to carry out the work organised by the teacher, but in some you may be teaching a small group some aspect of the subject or developing a theme that the teacher has introduced. There will often be opportunities for discussion with a small group of children, helping them to understand further the work of the class.

Case study 11.1

Juliet was a teaching assistant working with a Year 6 class. She came to the post after spending a year in Japan with her husband, who worked for a Japanese company operating in England and who was spending a year with the parent company to get to know the way they worked. When they came back Juliet saw a teaching assistant's job advertised and applied for it. She was delighted to be appointed as she loved children and wanted to work with them.

When Yvonne, the class teacher, heard about her Japanese experience, she decided that the class would do a project on Japan, based on some of what Juliet could tell them. They looked at the map of the world and saw where Japan was and Juliet then told them a number of interesting things about the Japanese.

She described the way Japanese people bowed to each other when they were introduced. She said it was difficult to get used to at first, but quite soon she was bowing away with everyone else. They were very polite to each other. She told them how people took off their shoes when they entered someone's house or a building. She had to take off her shoes when she visited a school and was provided with a kind of loose slipper to put on. People also sat on the floor a lot, even sometimes to eat. She told them about the way Japanese people used chopsticks rather than a knife and fork and she brought some pieces of apple and three pairs of chopsticks into the classroom for some children to try. They found it very difficult but enjoyed the attempt.

She talked about the way Japanese people wrote, which was different from our way of forming words from letters. Instead they drew signs, which represented ideas perhaps of several words at a time. There were about 3,000 of these to learn. She showed them a Japanese newspaper and passed round two books she had brought back.

She then went on to talk about schools in Japan, where children worked very hard. They also were responsible for cleaning their schools, which did not employ cleaners. One result of this was that Japanese people tended to be very tidy. The streets were clean and free of rubbish, because children had learned to clear up after themselves at school.

She also had a videotape she had made during her stay in Japan, which showed what the streets looked like and some of the sights, including some shots of people in national costume.

They very much enjoyed all this and it made a good starting point for finding out more.

A school should try to make good use of any special knowledge or skills that you bring to your work. You may have particular knowledge and skills in some of the subjects and the class teacher should make good use of these, so make sure that s/he knows what you can offer.

In addition to the work laid down by the National Curriculum in each subject, every school will have its own schemes of work for each subject for each age group, based on the National Curriculum, and you will gradually become familiar with these as you work with the class teacher.

Questions for consideration

1   Have I any particular skills or knowledge that could be useful? Does the school and the class teacher know about these?

2   What subjects do I know least about? Could I prepare for these by looking at the materials the children are using?

3   Have I access to the schemes of work that apply to the class I work with? Do I understand them? Do I need to ask the teacher to explain some of the statements in them?

4   Does the teacher I work with arrange any project work for the children? How can I contribute to this?

Chapter 12

Managing behaviour

Control of children in the classroom is the responsibility of the classroom teacher, but s/he will want you to back up her attempts to create a classroom atmosphere in which children behave well and can learn. Classroom teachers usually have a set of rules in mind when insisting on certain behaviour. These may not be made explicit but can usually be deduced from listening to the comments the teacher makes about behaviour and the things s/he scolds children for doing or not doing. You need to keep these rules in mind when working with groups of children or individuals. You will also need to keep the class teacher informed about your observations of children who tend to misbehave and the effects of different strategies for improving behaviour.

Behaviour problems

As a teaching assistant you will, of course, be able to refer children who misbehave to the teacher, but you need first to do your best to control the behaviour of the children with whom you work. As a newly appointed teaching assistant you may naturally be apprehensive about possible misbehaviour, but as you get to know the children you will gradually work out the best way to get and maintain their attention and get them to concentrate on their learning.

There are a number of situations that you are likely to encounter and you need to work out ways of dealing with them. Older children, in particular, may test out how far they can go with you and you will need to be clear about the limits of what you will allow. There may be children who find it difficult to concentrate and are disturbing to other children. You may encounter rudeness, swearing or over-familiarity. There may be examples of antisocial behaviour. You need to be sensitive to non-verbal signs. A certain restlessness and inability to sit still may lead to misbehaviour. Reluctance to make eye contact and facial tensions may signal unwillingness to cooperate. There may be an attempt to get an audience from other children rather than working with you. Children may argue with each other and with you. Young children may show temper tantrums. All these are ways in which children show their unreadiness to cooperate. They are all problems that you can learn to deal with.

There will also be differences in the behaviour of different groups of children. Boys and girls tend to behave differently and respond to things differently. Girls tend to have lower self-esteem than boys and to be more ready to behave well. They are generally better at English and boys are better at mathematics. Boys tend to be more restless and are more likely to create behaviour problems. Afro-Caribbean boys, in particular, sometimes find difficulty with school work and react against this by misbehaving. Children from disadvantaged areas tend to have lower self-esteem and this may affect their behaviour.

Causes of misbehaviour

It is important to try to understand why a child misbehaves. There may be a home problem, which is occupying the child's thoughts and making it difficult to concentrate on school work. A child may have difficulty in relating to adults, perhaps not understanding someone's body language. This may be a particular problem for children from some ethnic minority families, for whom the body language current in British society may be unfamiliar. This may be particularly the case with the younger children who have yet to learn our body language.

Low self-esteem often leads to misbehaviour because the child may look for a way of getting the attention of the peer group. If you are dealing with a group who have learning difficulties, there may be children, particularly boys, who feel themselves to be failures and have concluded that it isn't worth trying.

Dealing with misbehaviour

Just as the teacher has a set of rules about behaviour, which may or may not be explicit, you need to think about what you will find acceptable and unacceptable and let the children know about this. Watch the teacher with the children and note the rules s/he is applying. Would any of these be the same for you or would you be more strict or more lenient?

It has been said that expecting bad behaviour is a sure way of getting it. You need to start out with high and positive expectations for behaviour as well as performance and communicate this to children by making positive comments about the way you expect them to behave, and praising the behaviour you want to establish, rather than commenting too much on the kind of behaviour you don't want. It will, of course, be necessary to comment on such behaviour from time to time, but try to do this in a positive way, saying, for example, 'You usually concentrate on your work better than this, John. Show me that you haven't forgotten how to do that.' Your aim should be to establish the idea that a child's misbehaviour is a digression from his or her usual behaviour, thus helping them to see themselves as good workers and well-behaved children. The same thing applies when dealing with rudeness or swearing. It is important to keep calm or at least to behave as though you felt calm and say something like 'I'll pretend I didn't hear that, Janet. It's unlike you to say things like that.' Whenever you tackle a piece of misbehaviour, make it clear that it is the behaviour that you don't like, not the person.

With children who have low self-esteem you will need to work to improve their view of themselves. They will be anxious and tend to lack enthusiasm for their work and you need to praise them wherever you can and look for small steps that they can take successfully. You need to win their trust and show that you care for them and believe that they can succeed, demonstrating that you have high expectations of them and will help them to reach your goals for them and the targets they may perhaps have agreed with the teacher.

Children can sometimes be led into misbehaviour by having other children as an audience or they may perhaps take advantage of a situation in which there is a lot of movement to help to create chaos by misbehaving. One theory about classroom discipline suggests that you look for the antecedents of a piece of misbehaviour to help you to understand why it occurred. This can help you to avoid such a situation next time. You can also do what is called shaping behaviour. In this you look for any sign of the behaviour you want and praise it in the hope that it will be repeated.

You then praise the child for repeating the desired behaviour and look for other signs of improvement, praising those as they occur. This enables you to help a child change his or her behaviour in a gradual way.

Case study 12.1

Geoffrey suffered from Attention Deficit Hyperactivity Disorder (**ADHD**). He was impulsive and disorganised and made careless mistakes. He was also a nuisance in class because he had difficulty staying in his seat or staying with a piece of work. Lesley was an LSA in his Year 3 class and was responsible for supporting him. This was quite a difficult responsibility because he did not respond very well to her help. She often discussed the problem with the school SENCO as well as with the class teacher. The SENCO suggested that she set up a very regular routine for Geoffrey and did her best to make him stick to it. She should also look for ways of shaping his behaviour, helping him and praising him when he showed any sign of becoming more organised and ready to tackle his work.

Lesley did these things and also had an idea about improving his ability to concentrate. She talked with him about the need to improve his concentration and suggested that she would bring in a timer and set it to sound in 10 minutes, with the idea that Geoffrey would aim to sit in his place and concentrate on his work for that amount of time. If he could concentrate for three lots of 10 minutes in a row, she would give him a star to stick on a special chart she had made for him. She talked this over with the class teacher who agreed that, if he won an agreed number of stars in a fortnight, she would write a letter to his parents saying how well he had done.

He was quite enthusiastic about this idea. His parents had made it clear that they were worried about his inability to work in school and he minded this although he pretended it didn't matter. This meant that a letter home praising him was really important to him and was a good incentive to make him concentrate.

This worked quite well and the teacher was able to write to his parents after a month. Lesley then made the task a bit harder with a longer time of concentration needed to get a star and a letter home.

Gradually he became rather better at concentrating and everyone seemed to be pleased with him, which was a change for him.

When you are going round the class in order to help anyone who needs you, rather than working with individuals or small groups, look out for children getting ready to misbehave, perhaps whispering to someone sitting near them or looking round the room rather than working. It is important to know children's names in this context, as calling a child by his or her name makes more impact. You can often deal with this kind of incipient misbehaviour by asking if the child in question needs any help or asking a question about how s/he is tackling the work in hand.

It is surprisingly easy to label children and many teachers find it difficult to avoid doing this because they are dealing with a large number of children and labelling can seem to help to make the job easier. It is important to try to see the children as individuals,

---

Helping children to manage their behaviour

Start by helping children to develop good social skills. How well do they work in a group? Do they like group work? What do they think makes for good group work? Get them to think about how to make the group work well, with people listening to each other, helping each other and being ready to help other people develop their ideas as well as wanting to contribute their own. Help them to express their feelings about something in a way that doesn't upset other people. Discuss with them how a particular piece of group work succeeded or failed.

It is also helpful to discuss what makes them misbehave. Are they bored? What would make them behave more sensibly? What ways of working do they enjoy most? How can they make themselves work at things that don't interest them much – given that there will always be things, such as tables, that are a bit boring to learn but useful when learned.

each with his or her own background, particular skills and qualities and to work with them on that basis. Black Afro-Caribbean boys sometimes tend to be labelled as troublemakers and their behaviour is sometimes misinterpreted because their culture accepts and expects behaviour that is different from that of other ethnic groups and white children. Very able children are sometimes underestimated. One piece of research found that very able children were often given work that was much too easy for them. Children from disadvantaged homes or with poor speech are also underestimated from time to time, because the culture they bring from home is different from that of the school. You need to be aware of these pitfalls and you have the advantage that you will often be working with quite small groups in which you can get to know the children's abilities and preferences really well.

You will need to agree with your class teacher how s/he would like you to act if a child continues to pose a problem that you feel you can't handle. Your class teacher will use both rewards and sanctions from time to time and you will want to know if there are situations where you could use a particular penalty for bad behaviour. By and large it is better to avoid sanctions as much as possible because they only have a limited and rather short-lived effect. You probably already know that any form of physical punishment in schools is illegal, but your class teacher may use team points for rewards and a loss of these as a sanction and you may be allowed to use this scheme. Rewarding good behaviour is always better and more effective than punishment of bad behaviour.

Questions for consideration

1   What rules for behaviour does my class teacher have? Are these explicit and made known to the children or simply implied in what the teacher praises and discourages?

2   What underlying rules should I have for working with children?

3   What sorts of misbehaviour am I encountering? How should I deal with it? Am I aware of non-verbal signs of incipient misbehaviour?

4   Am I dealing with any children who have problems at home that are affecting their work in school? How can I best deal with this?

5   Am I dealing with problems of behaviour in a positive way, making it clear that it is the behaviour I dislike, not the child?

6   Am I labelling any children rather than studying them as individuals?

7   Do I know what to do in the case of a child who poses more of a problem than I can manage? Am I allowed to use any rewards and sanctions?

8   What am I doing to help children become better learners?

Chapter 13

The learning environment

The National Occupational Standards for Teaching Assistants say that teaching assistants should help to prepare the learning environment and monitor and maintain it. Teachers will welcome the support in such tasks as setting out play equipment for young children, preparing the resources for particular lessons, perhaps cutting paper to size, sharpening pencils, arranging equipment ready for children to use, photocopying, seeing that things go back to their right places after use and generally looking after materials and equipment, perhaps involving children in some of these tasks. It will also be important to know about safety issues, particularly in a subject like technology where you will need to help children to use equipment safely. You should be familiar with the school health and safety policy, the drill in case of accidents and the whereabouts of the first-aid box.

Caring for resources

You may be asked to organise the learning materials in your classroom so that children can find them, use them and return them to their rightful places. In the nursery and reception classes, you will need to see that there is a place for each item of equipment and label this with a drawing or diagram of what should be there. The teacher will no doubt have rules about the number of children who can play in a given area and use particular equipment. As children grow older you can label spaces with words. You then need to check over the shelves and worktops where things are stored to see that everything is in its right place and also to check if anything needs repair or replacement. Look for suitable containers for small items such as pencils, rulers, set squares, paint brushes, paints, scissors, and so on. Jam jars make good containers for pencils and brushes, and you can collect suitable boxes for scissors and other equipment. Many things, such as shoes and chocolates, are sold in boxes that can be used.

Case study 13.1

Karah, who was a teaching assistant in a Year 4 class, worked hard to get the classroom resources organised but was somewhat frustrated to find at the end of each day that her carefully arranged shelves and worktops were in a muddle, in spite of the fact that everything was clearly labelled.

She talked this over with Ken, the class teacher, who was sympathetic because he had experienced the same problem. He suggested that they should look for a way of involving the children more in caring for the resources. Karah thought about this and suggested giving children, in pairs, the task of checking a particular shelf or worktop space labelled with their names as well as the titles of the equipment that should be there and then, at the end of the day, giving them the task of checking their shelves and reporting if anything was in the wrong place or missing.

Ken liked this idea and asked Karah to organise it. She explained to the children what they had to do and suggested they should also look to see if anything had been broken or damaged and report this to her. The children were keen to take part and Karah labelled each shelf or part of a worktop with the names of the pairs of children and asked them to look and see what was there and how it was arranged.

At the end of the first day, the teacher told the children to go and check their spaces. They did this carefully and were able to report on two worksheets that had become torn. When Karah checked over the shelves herself she found that everything was in place and she congratulated the children on their good work.

The scheme continued to work satisfactorily, with very few occasions when things were not in place. The children became very good about chasing up their peers to return things to the right place and reporting things that were damaged or broken.

Be prepared for making displays

Keep a box of the things you may want to use to display work on a display board – double-sided sellotape, ruler, drawing pins and a stapler and staples, or a pushpin device for attaching things to a display board with sewing pins. You will also need ready access to a guillotine. Use the computer to provide names or information about what is being displayed, so that you provide good-looking labels and use lettering large enough to be seen from a distance.

Another task that will fall to you is the mounting and display of children's work. The teacher will usually wish to select the work to be displayed, sometimes wanting the best work on show and sometimes wanting to encourage less able children by displaying theirs. Whether you are mounting writing or art work you need to arrange things so that there is a larger margin at the bottom than the top. It is also sometimes a good idea to double-mount art work using a background mount that gives a margin round the work of a colour that looks well with the work. Another possibility is to cover an area of wall with coloured sheets of paper as a background for work. Double-sided sellotape is useful for sticking work to mounts.

Sometimes a teacher will want a display of photographs or newspaper cuttings about a particular theme and children may perhaps bring things in to include. These can be mounted in a similar way to children's work. There may also be occasions for three-dimensional displays, when children have been modelling in clay or plasticine or making things from scrap materials. Open shelving is useful for this or you can make a kind of stand from a large cardboard box, covering it with coloured paper or fabric.

Questions for consideration

1 Are the resources in my classroom arranged so that children can access them and return them to the right place easily? Are they clearly labelled so that it is easy to return them to the right place? Does the system work satisfactorily?

2 What responsibility for resources does my class teacher want me to undertake?

3 Am I familiar with the school health and safety policy and do I know what to do if a child has an accident? Do I know where the first-aid box is kept?

4 Have I the equipment to mount displays? Is it easily accessible?

5 Have we got a place for three-dimensional displays?

Chapter 14

Providing for all children

Each child is unique and different. S/he comes to school from a background from which s/he has already learned a good deal. Infant school teachers have the difficult job of trying to provide for a class of children who all have different amounts of knowledge already, different learning abilities and styles, and different cultural and social backgrounds. Schools must do their best to provide equal opportunities for learning for all children, regardless of all these differences. Your school should have an equal opportunities policy and you should make yourself familiar with this.

The teacher tries to find out as much as s/he can about all these issues in order to provide teaching and learning opportunities that match as many children as possible. You can be very helpful in this difficult task by contributing the evidence you are picking up with another pair of eyes and ears. Your observations and the things you have learned from talking with different children will all be useful when you talk over the children's progress with the teacher.

Gender differences

The first difference between children is that of gender. Boys and girls develop at different rates and learn differently. For most of the time in the primary school, boys are developmentally behind girls by a small margin. They also tend to have different attitudes to learning. Most boys like being active and are less enthusiastic about reading and writing than girls. However, they are more enthusiastic about mathematics, science, ICT and technology and are often better at these subjects than girls, who tend to outperform boys at English. Boys tend to be risk-takers, whereas girls will be more likely to choose the safe option. When the teacher asks a question of the class, it is usual for more boys' hands to be raised than girls' hands. They are more likely to risk being wrong.

Even in the nursery boys and girls tend to play with different toys and boys are often more active than girls. One study of their play showed that, when a boy or girl was playing alone, s/he would sometimes play with toys usually preferred by the opposite sex, but, when another child joined in, the first child would revert to so-called gender-appropriate toys. As children grow older the tendency for play to be sex-stereotyped becomes more marked. Boys use constructional play more, with such things as bricks, cars and trains, whereas girls play in the Wendy house or home corner and doll's house. Girls also tend to like school better than boys, possibly because they tend to make faster progress.

There is a sort of hidden curriculum about the treatment of boys and girls in school. People sometimes tend to have different views about boys and girls that may not always be justifiable. There can be a tendency in some schools to attribute poor performance in boys to lack of effort and motivation and in girls to lack of ability. Girls tend to have less confidence in their abilities than boys, perhaps as a result of becoming conscious of such views.

At the same time boys tend to get more disapproval and critical comments from their teachers, who, probably because of their general restlessness and tendency to misbehaviour, are inclined to give more attention to boys than to girls. Boys often get more chances to answer questions in class than girls.

Boys tend to be more outspoken, they call out in class, have more to say than girls and consequently receive more attention from teachers. They are often disparaging of girls and tend to dominate and get more than their fair share of the resources available and leave the girls to do the clearing up.

Of course, there are always boys who don't fit these descriptions, who work diligently and are good at English and who are less enthusiastic about mathematics and science, while there are girls who excel in these subjects. All generalisations need to be considered carefully while looking for the exceptions.

These differences are all things that you can notice and perhaps note when observing children. Do the boys dominate in any group you work with? Do boys put their hands up in answer to questions more often than girls in the class you work with? Is the teacher more critical of boys than girls and do you think this is justified? Can you do anything to help boys and girls to work together more and learn from each other?

In planning work for a group that contains some boys or planning for an individual boy, it is helpful to remember that boys like definite things to do with a foreseeable end-point. They like being active in their thoughts as well as physically. They also enjoy working with others. They like competition if they feel they have a chance of winning or succeeding and they enjoy the competitive element in quizzes and questionnaires. They like to talk and don't much like writing. They also enjoy ICT. It is important in catering for the boys not to forget the girls, who tend to be easier to provide for. Girls enjoy many of the things that boys do, so providing for them is not difficult. The boys tend to be more demanding, so you need to try to see that you give the girls a fair amount of attention.

Special educational needs (SEN)

Work with children who have SEN is guided by the **Code of Practice**. This is a government document that sets out how such children should be identified and supported. Part of that support for those whose needs are very demanding is the appointment of an LSA. If you are a general teaching assistant you will also be likely to be concerned with some children with SEN, because they tend to be the children who need the most help. Schools must not discriminate against children with SEN and must make provision for their learning and involvement in all the activities of the school. The school must have a written SEN policy and you should make yourself familiar with this.

The *Code* states that, if a child's rate of progress is inadequate, it will be necessary to take some action to enable the child to learn more effectively. The SENCO and the child's teacher, together with the parents, should decide upon the action to be taken to help the child to make progress. Plans should be made for an IEP for the child, which includes information about the short-term targets and the provision that is to be put in place. This may be some individual support from a teaching assistant or LSA, or the provision of different learning materials or special equipment, and the results of this intervention should be carefully monitored.

If the child continues to make little progress, it will be time to seek outside help. The school or the parents can ask the LEA for a statutory assessment, which may lead to a Statement of SEN. This will specify what is to be done to help the child, and what additional resources will be made available for this. This is the point at which an LSA may be appointed. A further IEP will be worked out and plans put into action and monitored with the teacher and the SENCO, and if you are an LSA you will probably be involved in these decisions.

The causes of SEN may be mental difficulties, poor communication skills, inadequate perceptual or motor skills, physical disabilities, emotional and behaviour problems, social skills or a combination of these. Parents should be fully consulted at all stages and older children, too, should be consulted. The SENCO should discuss with you what has been found out about the child and brief you on the planning for his or her support. The SENCO will be responsible for the programme overall and, with the class teacher, will tell you the kinds of records you need to keep of the child's progress. In working with such a child it is helpful at an early stage to get the child's own views of his or her difficulties.

Case study 14.1

Angela suffered from dyslexia. She was now aged 7 and in Year 2 and found reading and writing very difficult. She tended to get letters in the wrong order in words and had difficulty in remembering which letters stood for which sounds. She was disorganised and forgot and lost things. She had had a Statement of SEN since Year 1.

Tricia was an LSA appointed to help Angela and she had been supporting her since Year 1, so they knew each other very well and Tricia was very sensitive to Angela's needs and had helped her a good deal over this period. Together they made up stories to help Angela remember how to spell words. For example 'Which House is Colin's House' was used as a way to remember the word 'which' and 'Sister Christine Has Only One Leg' for 'school'. Angela really enjoyed this and found that she could get the words they did this with right every time.

Tricia also encouraged Angela to trace words in the air while saying the letters to herself, so that the memory of the movement might help her to remember. She also got her to look for words within words; for example, she pointed out that the word 'important' was made up of three bits – 'im', 'port' and 'ant' and she could remember it by thinking about an ant bringing a boat into port.

They also read together, reading a sentence each and periodically stopping to talk about what might happen next. This helped Angela to make sense of what she was reading because the reading flowed more quickly. When Angela got stuck on a word, Tricia might suggest first looking at the letters to see if she could work it out from the spelling, then, if she couldn't get it, looking at the whole sentence again to see if she could guess. If she still couldn't get it, Tricia would give her a clue, perhaps breaking the word down into parts.

Tricia kept a record of the words that Angela found difficult in reading and those she misspelt. She wrote ten of these words on pieces of cards and made a word box for them. There was a short time each day when Tricia worked with Angela, helping her with reading and spelling, and each day they worked through the cards with Angela reading as many of the words as she could. Then they closed the box and Tricia dictated them to her and she wrote them down. She then checked what she had written against the words in the box and they talked about ways of remembering those she couldn't read or spelled wrongly. When she could read and write all the words correctly Tricia added some more and so gradually built up a vocabulary.

There was a very good relationship between Tricia and Angela, and Angela made good progress partly as a result of Tricia's patient help.

Exceptional ability

Every so often a class contains a child who is very able indeed. Such children are usually reading very early, often before they start school. They ask interesting questions and are keen to learn. They often have plenty to say and write at length, though their work is often untidy because their thoughts move more quickly than they can get their ideas down. They may have difficulty in making friends because their age contemporaries are not interested in the same things as they are. They may also become a bit embarrassed at finding themselves finishing work more quickly than other children and getting praise from the teacher for interesting work. As a result they may hide their abilities in order to keep in line with their peers and deliberately underachieve. There may also be children in the class you work with who have talents in music, art or movement skills and games and you need to look out for these and help the teacher to find ways of helping them to develop their talents.

There is a sense in which teachers need to look for particular abilities in all children and foster them, but this is not easy given the numbers in the average class. The class teacher will probably be well aware of really able children and will try, as far as it is possible, to find work that will stimulate them. You may be able to help with identifying such children and help the teacher to find stimulating work for them. In talking to a child you may hear about particular interests or ideas that, with encouragement, could lead to interesting work. You will probably have some opportunities to talk with individual children and find out what they do in their spare time and what interests them most, and this can lead to some individual work if the teacher agrees.

Case study 14.2

Joseph was in Year 2 where Miranda was a teaching assistant. She noticed that he read very fluently and, in conversation with him, she discovered that at home he read books far more advanced than those he was reading in school. For example, he said he had read *Oliver Twist* after seeing the musical *Oliver!* on television. Miranda questioned him about the book and found he really appeared to have read it and enjoyed it. She talked to Muriel, the class teacher, about this and found her really surprised by this news. They went on to talk about how to find work for him that would really make demands. He did all the work of the class very adequately, but Muriel had not previously been fully aware of how far beyond the majority Joseph appeared to be.

They decided to get him to consider writing a substantial piece of work – an autobiography that would give them some clues about his interests. Miranda talked to Joseph about this idea and explained what an autobiography was and asked him whether he would be interested in doing this. He was quite enthusiastic about it and Muriel suggested that he wrote it on computer so that he could print out a fair copy. Miranda discussed with him what he might include, starting with what his parents could tell him about his early years and going on to his time in nursery and reception and Year 1. He could also include details of his interests and what he liked doing at home and at school.

The autobiography was a great success. He printed out a 15-page booklet and designed a cover. The work was then stapled together to form a book, which he took home to show his parents.

Finding work demanding enough for Joseph continued to be a problem that Muriel and Miranda enjoyed trying to solve.

Ethnic minorities

Many schools today have children from a range of cultures, some of whom do not speak English at home. The group of ethnic minority children may include children from widely differing cultures. Many will be of Asian origin, some may be Afro-Caribbean and there may also be Chinese children and children from a number of different countries. The more you can find out about the cultures of these different groups the better, since it will make you aware of the children's out-of-school experience. This is particularly important with the younger children, who will be trying to come to terms with the culture of the school, particularly if they don't speak much English.

All of us have ideas about other cultures and some of these ideas are racist. It is easy to have expectations about children, particularly ethnic minority children, which are too low or too high and this is something to guard against. It is important that all staff in a school see children as individuals and value them and teach children to value each other and other people. In some cases, indigenous children may come from homes where the parents are racist and this can perhaps make the children unsympathetic to children of other races. It is important to use any opportunity that occurs to emphasise the importance of valuing all people for what they are and to emphasise the need to be sensitive to others because racist comments are upsetting to other people. This may be particularly important in a school where there are few children from other cultures. You need to fight prejudice wherever you find it. Today's children are growing up in an ethnically mixed society and need to develop positive views about people of other cultures, valuing them as individuals.

There are considerable differences between children of different races in the progress they make in school. Some of them start at a disadvantage because English is not their mother tongue.

English as a second language

Children who have English as a second language need you to use extra body language to help them understand, such as gestures, pointing and facial expression. Speak slowly and limit the range of language you use, introducing new words very slowly, with plenty of repetition and, if possible, in a context that helps understanding. Use visual material, objects and pictures. Try to correct mistakes indirectly, perhaps by repeating the child's expressions correctly in the form of a reply. Remember that you are a role model for language and try to enunciate clearly. Check the children's understanding from time to time so that you get a picture of the amount of English that individuals are able to understand and use and give plenty of praise and encouragement.

However, such children usually make good progress once they have mastered the new language and then have the advantage of being bilingual and at home in more than one language. Asian children often do well, although Pakistani and Bangladeshi children tend to lag behind. Black Afro-Caribbean children, boys in particular, start school more or less level with their age group, but as they move through the primary school they tend to get further and further behind and do not catch up in the secondary school. Schools should keep records of the achievement of each ethnic group so that they can support groups who appear to do less well.

Differences in social background

There are differences in the home background of children that affect the knowledge, skills and ability they bring to school learning. In particular there are substantial differences in reading performance between children of different social classes. This is probably because some children have books at home, are read to as small children, and see their parents reading, while others have few books and do not see parents reading much.

Research has suggested that the kinds of conversations with children that take place at home make a difference to a child's thinking. While working-class and middle-class parents talk with their children to roughly the same extent, giving them information of many kinds, middle-class mothers tend to use more complex language and cover a larger range of topics, using a wider range of vocabulary than working-class mothers.

Differences probably also occur according to the interest parents have in education and the extent to which they endeavour to see that their children see it as important, encourage them in school learning and provide learning experiences at home. Black parents tend to do a good deal to support their children's schooling and this isn't always appreciated by teachers.

It is very easy to make judgements about children's backgrounds because of the way they speak. A child who speaks with a local accent or ungrammatically is often judged to be less able and this may not be the case. Your own speech will be important as an example and, while you will want to try to get such children to improve their speech, this needs to be done very tactfully. A person's speech is part of their personality and connects them to their home and family and boys, in particular, may not want to change the way they speak.

Questions for consideration

1   What different groups of children are there in the class in which I work?

2   What provision does the teacher make to meet the needs of all children? What can I do to help?

3   Are boys and girls treated differently in the class I work with? Do I find myself treating them differently when I work with a group? Are these differences justified?

4   How many children are there in the class who have SEN? How many have Statements? What can I do to help them?

5   Are there any exceptionally able children in the class? What makes me come to this conclusion about an individual child? Can I do anything to help such children?

6   Are there any children from ethnic minorities in the class? How many have English as a second language? How can I help them?

7   Do I assume that children who don't speak standard English are less able than those who do? Is this view justified?

Chapter 15

Evaluation and record-keeping

Your class teacher will be continually assessing how well children are progressing, how much they understand and can do, the difficulties individuals are encountering and many other things. This kind of assessment is needed in order to decide on what to teach next and what needs to be done for children who are not making good progress by comparison with their earlier work and also for those who show that they are more able than the majority. It will be particularly important to assess regularly the progress of children with SEN and the very able in order to decide what should be tackled next.

The teacher may also want to compare groups in the class, for example the performance and progress of boys and girls, or children of different abilities or different ethnic backgrounds. Assessment is also necessary in order to report progress to parents and to provide reports for the next teacher or school when children change classes or schools at the end of the school year. Where the teacher is trying a new approach or tackling a new project with the class s/he will want to test how successful the experiment has been. The teacher will also be keeping various kinds of records of children's performance and progress and will want you to contribute to these.

You will be in a strong position to help with this process, particularly for the children with whom you are working, but also for all the children, whom you will often be observing while the teacher works with the whole class. You need to talk with the teacher and find out the things s/he would like you to look out for, and also the things that you should record and share. You will also want to make observations for your own benefit to decide how best to help any children with whom you are working.

Types of assessment and evaluation

The words evaluation and assessment are frequently used as if they were interchangeable. In fact, there is a difference. You assess in order to gain information so that you can evaluate a situation and so decide what to do next.

There are various types of assessment. It can be formative, as when you assess in order to help while a child is in the process of working at something and you or the teacher comes along and suggests a new idea or a way of developing the work further. It can also be summative, as when you or the teacher talks with the child when the work is completed and reviews what the child has done, or when the teacher marks a piece of work and makes a comment on it.

Assessment may also be long- or short-term. A teacher may assess a child's progress over a term or year when writing a report for the child's parents, the next teacher or school. The majority of assessments will be short-term, assessing what happened today or during the last week.

Children should also be encouraged to assess their own work and progress. It is a good idea, when discussing a piece of work with a child, to start by asking what s/he thought about it. Was s/he pleased with the outcome? In what ways could it have been better? Did s/he enjoy doing it? Was there anything particularly difficult about doing this piece of work? It is also sometimes helpful to get children to assess each other's work. This alerts them to what they should look out for and you can discuss this with them so that they learn through this activity for their own work.

Suggestions for assessing your own work

Do you go over what you have done during the day, asking yourself what went well and why it went well, so that you can learn from it for future occasions? Was there any way in which you feel you could have done better? What things do you find particularly difficult? What do you think are your strengths and are you making the most of them? Are you getting better at the job as time passes?

The processes of assessment and evaluation

What is actually involved in the process of assessing and evaluating? You need to think about why you are making an assessment. The answer will quite often be that the teacher has asked you to do this, but you will also want to assess for your own information, so that you can think what you might do next with a child or group of children and so that you can assess how effective you have been. It is useful to give yourself criteria for assessment. For example, you might plan a way to get a slow-learning child whom you have been helping to understand the sums that the class has been learning about to show his or her understanding by doing three examples correctly. You will find this difficult at first because you need to learn about children's problems in understanding new work, but, as you get more experienced, this kind of target becomes a possibility. You then assess whether the child achieved as you planned.

The next task is to think about the evidence you and the teacher have for assessment and evaluation. The teacher will often discuss this with you so that you can look for the information s/he needs to know how the children are doing. Evidence can be of the following types.

Observation

You will have many chances to observe children and the teacher will probably have ideas s/he would like you to look out for when s/he is working with the class. You may also have ideas of your own. For example, you may like to check on how many boys and how many girls actually have the chance to answer questions. You may also like to note how many children were really involved in what the class was doing and how many were dreaming or wasting their time in some way. There is an advantage in sitting at one side at the front of the class when the teacher is teaching so that you can see the children's faces and get clues about their thinking. You can also learn a lot about children's physical skills when watching PE or games.

When you are working with a group you will be looking for the children's body language, which tells you whether or not they are interested and concentrating on the work in hand, or that a child would like to ask a question or doesn't understand what you are saying. Observation will be particularly important if you work in a nursery. You can watch the activities a child does, how s/he gets on with other children, how long the child stays with any particular activity, what s/he is learning from it, what s/he is able to do and understand, the child's attitudes to various activities and to other children and adults and the level of communication the child has developed.

Case study 15.1

Joy particularly enjoyed talking with the children in her Year 1 class. They had all sorts of ideas that they didn't express in class and they welcomed her as a ready listener. She appreciated that she had more opportunities for talking with the children and listening to what they said than the teacher who had the whole class to listen to, and she encouraged them to tell her about all sorts of things. They told her about their homes and families, about things they did at the weekend, the work they found interesting and the work that they disliked, the problems they were encountering and their quarrels with friends. She always tried to draw them out because she felt that the more she knew about them the better she could help them learn.

One member of the class who often talked to her on the way home from school, because he lived near her, was Jimmy. Jimmy had a stammer and took a long time to say things, so the walk home with Joy, without other children interrupting, was a welcome opportunity for him to talk about the frustration he felt at not being able to say what he wanted when he wanted. Other children tended to make fun of him and he could never answer in class because he couldn't get the words out quickly enough. Joy used this opportunity to encourage him and talk about her sister who had had a stammer as a child and eventually overcame it to a large extent and went on to have an important job when she grew up. Jimmy found this encouraging and often asked questions about her sister. This opportunity to talk about his frustration helped him a good deal and he became less self-conscious about his stammer, though he couldn't cure it.

You will also be listening to what children say to check their understanding of the work. Try to ask short questions that encourage children to tell you more and follow up replies with further questions when this seems appropriate. The teacher will welcome this kind of information because it helps him or her to match work to children more effectively.

Children's work

The next area that gives you information is the children's work. You will probably be able to get a picture of the range of abilities in the class by looking at individual exercise books, when you are helping either those who need extra help in class or those who have something to ask about. If the teacher has made comments on particular work you can get an impression of how far s/he thinks it is a true representation of the child's ability. You will get an impression about art work, technology designing and making and some other subjects when you put together displays of children's work.

One particular area in which you will learn a lot about the stage a child has reached is in hearing reading. You will be able to note the particular difficulties of individuals in this context, for example children whose phonic knowledge is weak, children who don't really understand what they are reading and children who haven't learned to make inferences from a text and understand what is implied but not actually said. You can check on these things when hearing a child read, not only by the places where s/he stumbles, but also by asking questions to check what has been understood.

Children's records

You can learn a lot about a child by studying the records of his or her progress and development over the years. The school must keep records for each child and you can ask to see these. The class teacher should also be prepared to let you see his or her records. This will be particularly important for children with SEN and the SENCO will probably be able to tell you a lot about such children, especially if a child has a Statement, and there will be a considerable amount of information about the various assessments that have been made and their implications for work with the child.

It is important to remember that school records of children are confidential. You must be very careful not to talk about a child's records to people outside the school, including parents, except where you know that they have already been informed of the material in question by the teacher or the SENCO. In case of doubt you should keep quiet.

Discussion with parents

If you work in a nursery you will have many opportunities to talk with parents about their children and this can tell you a good deal about the individual child. Parents can tell you what the child does at home, what s/he seems most interested in doing both at school and at home and how the parent feels the child is doing at nursery. Parents can also tell you about the place of the child in the family, his or her health and skills like dressing, toileting and using cutlery, and they can also raise any anxieties they may have. Make a point of talking with the teacher at an early stage about what you may discuss with parents about the progress of the child.

Case study 15.2

Gerald was a puzzle to Brenda Mitchell, his Year 5 class teacher. Linda, his Year 4 teacher, had told Brenda that Gerald was very intelligent and produced work of high quality and Brenda looked forward to teaching a bright boy. However, when Gerald came into her class he failed to live up to these predictions. He seemed morose and uninterested in almost everything. He did as little work as possible and rarely did his homework and when he did work it was careless and untidy. Brenda felt that something must have happened to him to account for this change and she wrote to his parents asking for a meeting. There was no reply to her letter. She tried talking to Gerald to see if she could find out the cause of this change, but he was not forthcoming. She talked over the whole problem with Wendy, her classroom assistant, and asked her if she would try to get Gerald to explain what was happening to him.

Gerald appeared to spend most playtimes and lunchtimes mooching round the playground, not joining in games with other boys, and Wendy thought it might be a good idea to go over and talk to him outside. She started with some obvious questions about why he had stopped working well, but got nowhere. Then she asked what his parents thought about this. He hesitated and then said gloomily, 'They just don't care about me.' She asked 'What did your Dad say when they got the letter from Mrs Mitchell?' Gerald said, 'He's not there now.' Wendy asked what he meant. 'He went off with some woman and my Mum's got her boyfriend living with us now. They're always kissing and cuddling and now my Mum's going to have a baby and she's got ever so fat. They haven't any time for me.' Wendy thought for a bit and then said, 'So that's why you aren't doing very well at school.' 'Yes,' said Gerald. 'Nobody cares about me any more.' There was a pause during which they both thought about the situation, then Wendy said, 'That's not true, you know. Mrs Mitchell and I care about you a lot and we want to help. I know life is difficult for you at the moment but have you ever thought about what you want to do when you grow up?' Gerald thought about this and then said 'I think I want to be a doctor.' They talked about this and Wendy told him he would have to work hard in school and learn enough to get to medical school and become properly qualified. He took this in and then said, 'I guess I'll have to think some more about things. I want to do better. Will you help me?' Wendy said, 'Of course. Come and talk with me whenever you feel miserable and we'll look for ways that I can help you.'

Of course, things didn't get better very quickly, but Gerald could be seen to make an effort and he often cornered Wendy to talk to her about the way things were at home. By the time he was ready for secondary school he was working well and still thinking about being a doctor.

Records and record-keeping

It will be important to find out at an early stage about the records that the teacher would like you to keep about the children with whom you work individually or in small groups. If you are an LSA, the SENCO will also want to see any records you make of the progress made by the child with whom you are working makes. You will also want to keep some records for your own benefit so that you can see how individual children have done over a period. Many records will serve both purposes.

Reading records

If you hear children read as part of your work you will need to keep careful records of how they are progressing. It is useful to note words a child stumbles over or has difficulty in reading so that you can later go over such words with the child and help him or her to learn them. It is also helpful to notice the way the child tackles words that are not immediately familiar. Does s/he use phonics to help and how well are they used? Is it clear that the child has the ability to sound out the letters of the word and build it up gradually? Does s/he do this accurately? Does s/he use the context of the word to guess at what it means? You also need to note whether the child reads with expression and understanding, perhaps asking questions about what a particular sentence meant and checking on understanding. Has the child skill in making inferences, understanding what is inferred but not actually said? Can s/he predict what might come next in the reading? You may also want to assess whether a child is on the right book. Is it too easy or too difficult? Can you recommend an appropriate change of reading material to the teacher?

More general records

You will also want to note how children are progressing in other activities as you work with them. It is a good idea to keep a loose-leaf file with a page for each child on which you note anything significant that occurs. You may find out about a child's home background and interests, and this may give you a pathway into finding activities that suit him or her. Note occasions when a child appears to be making a step forward in understanding or learning something. Notice the way a child communicates with you and with other children. Is s/he using language well? Are there occasions when his or her speech is poor and needs further development? If so, try to find a way of introducing a correct version in replying, rather than correcting the child. Speech is part of the personality and part of the home environment and correction may be seen as a personal attack. Where speech is far from standard English, it may be tactful to say that this is what we say in school and it is perfectly all right to speak differently at home and with your friends. However, swearing should always be checked.

Levels of achievement

Your class teacher may also want to keep a portfolio of work for each child so that s/he can make assessments to confirm the National Curriculum levels of achievement in each subject. These are set out in the National Curriculum and some information about them was given in the chapters on English, mathematics and science and the foundation subjects. This should enable you to help in the assessment of children's work. Each teacher has to assess children every year in every subject of the curriculum to report to parents. Towards the end of Year 2 the children take the SATs in English and mathematics and towards the end of Year 6 they take SATs in English, mathematics and science. The results of the Year 6 tests are sent on to secondary schools and are also reported to parents.

Personal records

It is a good idea to try to spend a few minutes at the end of each day to reflect on what has happened and ask yourself which things went well and which not so well and consider how you could improve the things that went not so well. You may like to discuss this with the class teacher if s/he is willing to spend the time with you. This will also give you some ideas for planning the next day's work. It may be a good idea to keep a diary of what happens day by day so that you can look back and learn from what has happened.

Questions for consideration

1   What records does the teacher want me to keep and what information does s/he want from me about the children with whom I am working? Does the SENCO want anything particular recorded about children with SEN?

2   Am I learning to assess children's work myself?

3   Do I have any criteria for evaluating children's work?

4   Do I encourage children to assess their own and each other's work?

5   What am I learning from observing children?

6   What am I learning from listening to them?

7   Have I an opportunity to see past records of children's progress, particularly those with SEN? Does my class teacher show me his or her records of children?

8   Am I keeping useful records of times when I hear children read?

9   Am I keeping useful records of children's progress and development in other subjects? Would it be helpful to use a computer for some of these?

Chapter 16

Professional development

All those who work in the field of education should regard themselves as learners. However much relevant experience and knowledge you bring to the job, there is always something new to learn. Every child is different and working with different children continually adds to your store of knowledge. Your learning can be informal or formal.

Informal learning opportunities

You will learn informally from many people and experiences. You will learn from observing teachers. This should give you ideas about how teachers manage control of children, how they talk to children, as a class and individually, how they introduce work and how they relate to individuals. You also learn from talking to teachers. Your class teacher will be able to give you feedback about how you are doing, especially if you show that you welcome his or her advice. S/he will provide opportunities to talk over your work and should be able to give you ideas about how to approach different work and deal with different children while you are learning about the job. You will also learn about the children from the teacher and from the teacher's records.

You will gradually gather knowledge about the best way to do your job as time goes on and be able to take on more difficult assignments. Other informal approaches to learning include the opportunity to be present at some meetings, such as meetings to discuss the teaching of a particular subject, meetings about a child with SEN or meetings with parents. The learning never stops and you need to take advantage of every opportunity to learn. This also makes you a good model for the children.

Helping children with SEN

If you work with children with SEN, talk to the school SENCO and get his or her advice as well as talking with the class teacher. The SENCO will have a great deal of information about individual children with SEN and may be able to suggest useful ways of working with different children. Talk with other LSAs and share ideas about ways of working with these children. Talk with the children to find out their interests and what makes them tick. This gives you useful information about how to approach particular pieces of learning.

Case study 16.1

Christine and Joanna were teaching assistants in the same school and worked in classrooms adjacent to each other. They also lived in the same area and when they got to know each other this led to their coming to school together in the same car. When coming and going they naturally talked about their work and this often involved sharing ideas and problems and helping each other with plans for the children. They both found this sharing very helpful and after a while they started to wonder whether the other teaching assistants in the school might welcome similar opportunities to discuss their work with each other. They thought a lot about this and eventually decided to ask the others if they would like to meet regularly one lunch hour each week to discuss their work. The others were quite enthusiastic about the idea and they talked to the head and their class teachers about the plan and met with an enthusiastic reception.

At the first meeting they agreed that they would take it in turns to chair the meeting. They discussed whether there should be minutes and this met with some opposition because of the time involved, but it was eventually agreed that someone should note any ideas that came up that everyone wanted to remember. They would take this task in turn, too.

The meetings went well and they were not only able to help each other a great deal but also were able to make suggestions about other things in the school. They suggested that there should be some regular training for teaching assistants, dealing with matters that gave them concern, such as child development and managing groups of children. They would also like to know more about computers and, in particular, how a computer might be used for their records of children. They suggested that they would like to be more involved when there were discussions about particular areas of the curriculum and suggested inviting each of the teachers who had a subject leadership role to a meeting so that they could learn more about each subject. They also decided that they would like to invite the SENCO to one of their meetings so that they might hear more about how the school was tackling children with SEN. The meeting became a valuable opportunity and they felt that it was time well spent.

Formal learning opportunities

There will also be some formal opportunities for learning. The school will have staff in-service days from which you can learn about current developments and approaches.

Case study 16.2

Jennifer was a bit alarmed when she was told about the school's performance management system. She was told that it involved having her work observed by the deputy head, followed by an opportunity to discuss it. This was worrying enough because she didn't feel very confident about the idea of someone looking critically at what she did. Her class teacher tried to encourage her, saying that she had found appraisal very helpful and thought Jennifer would, too, when she actually experienced it. She explained to Jennifer that she was expected to make an assessment of her own work, citing areas where she felt she was making progress and areas in which she would like to improve. Jennifer's first thought was that she would like to improve everything! Her class teacher also told her that she would be asked about Jennifer's work and that this would be a very positive report. She would also be asked about what professional development opportunities she would like and the areas in which she would like to learn more, and there would be an opportunity to discuss how her work was progressing more generally. She could also raise aspects of life in the school that she was not happy about in the hope that something could be done to help her. It was a real opportunity to review her work and she should get some positive feedback.

Jennifer took heart a little after the observation, which went well with the children responding to her and working steadily. When it came to the interview she had written down the things she wanted to say. She felt she had learned a lot in her first year in the school and she looked forward to getting better and better at the job as time went on. She felt her class teacher had been very helpful and that she had made good relationships with the children.

Marie, the deputy head, was a kind and sympathetic person who appreciated that the process was a bit alarming for someone experiencing it for the first time and she spoke in a very supportive way about Jennifer's progress, saying that she had done well in her first year and had been a real support to her class teacher. Marie asked her if there were areas in which she felt she needed to learn more. Jennifer said she felt that she lacked knowledge of the way children developed and learned and she needed to learn a lot more about ways of tackling difficult children, who tended to play her up if the class teacher allowed it. They talked about this and Marie made some suggestions that Jennifer found helpful. They went on to talk about the further training Jennifer would like and Marie told her about the NVQ courses that were available. Jennifer was keen to take such a course and Marie said she would try to arrange it.

Overall, Jennifer felt that she had had a useful and positive discussion that was a real help and nothing to worry about.

You may find that your school has a regular training programme for its teaching assistants, which addresses problems that are likely to be shared by all of you. Your LEA may run courses for teaching assistants, particularly the recently appointed. When you have settled comfortably into the job, you may like to discover other courses for teaching assistants. Local further education colleges are likely to run courses that will enable you to gain an NVQ in the work you actually do. There are NVQ qualifications at two levels, 2 and 3. These are based on National Occupational Standards for Teaching Assistants and are assessed on your actual work in the classroom, against clear statements about what you should actually be doing, and will be assessed by someone accredited as an assessor.

At level 2 teaching assistants must take four mandatory units and three optional units from a list of five. The mandatory units are:

2.1   Help with classroom resources and records.
2.2   Help with the care and support of pupils.
2.3   Provide support for learning activities.
2.4   Provide effective support for your colleagues.

The optional units are:

2.5   Support literacy and numeracy activities in the classroom.
3.1   Contribute to the management of pupils' behaviour.
3.1   Support the maintenance of pupils' safety and security.
3.10 Contribute to the health and well-being of pupils.
3.17 Support the use of ICT in the classroom.

NVQ level 3 has four mandatory units and nine optional units set out in four groups. Candidates have to choose one unit from each group and two others. It builds on level 2 in that some units are common to both levels and credit for them can be carried forward. The mandatory units are:

3.1   Contribute to the management of pupil behaviour.
3.2   Establish and maintain relationships with individual pupils and groups.
3.3   Support pupils during learning activities.
3.4   Review and develop your own professional practice.

The optional units are:

Set A
3.5   Assist in preparing and maintaining the learning environment.
3.6   Contribute to maintaining pupils' records.
3.7   Observe and report on pupil performance.
3.8   Contribute to the planning and evaluation of learning activities.

Set B

3.9 Promote pupils' social and emotional development.

3.10 Support the maintenance of pupil safety and security.

3.11 Contribute to the health and well-being of pupils.

3.12 Provide support for bilingual/multilingual pupils.

3.13 Support pupils with communication and interaction difficulties.

3.14 Support pupils with cognition and learning difficulties.

3.15 Support pupils with behavioural, emotional and social development needs.

3.16 Provide support for pupils with sensory and/or physical impairment.

Set C

3.17 Support the use of ICT in the classroom.

3.18 Help pupils to develop their literacy skills.

3.19 Help pupils to develop their numeracy skills.

3.20 Help pupils to access the curriculum.

Set D

3.21 Support the development and effectiveness of work teams.

3.22 Develop and maintain working relationships with other professionals.

3.33 Liaise effectively with parents.

All of these units at both levels have defined standards that the assistant has to demonstrate.

Questions for consideration

1   What opportunities for learning about the job are available to me both informally and formally?

2   What can I learn from observing my class teacher and the children?

3   What can I learn from discussion with the teacher, the SENCO, other teaching assistants, the children?

4   How can I best prepare for my performance management interview?

5   What courses are available to me in my area?

6   Do I want to gain a qualification in my work? Are there appropriate arrangements available in my area for this?

7   Do I undertake all the activities listed in the units for NVQ levels 2 and 3?

Chapter 17

Conclusion

As a teaching assistant you are part of a team and possibly more than one team. The basic team consists of you and your class teacher. You need to work closely together, sharing ideas and problems and planning together. This means spending some time each day reviewing the day's work and planning for the next day and also planning ahead. Your teacher will make the decisions about the work, but you will have opportunities not only to make suggestions but also to work out how best to carry out your part. This relationship is crucial to the success of the children in the class.

If you are an LSA, you may also be part of a team working with the SENCO as well as with class teachers. This will involve meeting regularly with the SENCO and perhaps with other LSAs as well as with class teachers. These meetings will provide good opportunities for giving and receiving information about the children in question and you will learn a good deal from discussion with other LSAs as you share problems.

Case study 16.1 in the last chapter suggested that there is a strong case for teaching assistants as a group regarding themselves as a team concerned with their own development and learning. If this is not recognised in your school it may be a good idea to suggest it. The school may have a higher-level teaching assistant who could lead such a team.

Being a teaching assistant is a very worthwhile job and you can feel that you are making a positive difference to the class you work with. Your presence enables the teacher to do much more to match learning opportunities to individual children. This is something that primary teachers have been attempting for years but have found difficult to do with large classes. The term 'personalised learning' is being used increasingly widely in national discussions and you are helping to make it a possibility in the primary school.

You may perhaps see this job as a step towards becoming a teacher yourself. It is a very worthwhile step towards such a goal and it will give you a good idea of what is involved in being a teacher and whether it is a job you would really enjoy. You will gain skills as a teaching assistant that will be invaluable in teaching because you will actually be doing a good deal of teaching as an assistant and you can get the feel of it and how satisfying it can be when things go well. You may also wish to go on to be a higher-level teaching assistant, perhaps working more in a leadership role. This requires NVQ level 3.

Every child is unique and different and this makes working with children always interesting and challenging. There is always something new to learn, new and interesting problems to solve and satisfaction when you can feel you have been able to do something to help a child learn.

Index

eBooks

eBooks – at www.eBookstore.tandf.co.uk

A library at your fingertips!

eBooks are electronic versions of printed books. You can store them on your PC/laptop or browse them online.

They have advantages for anyone needing rapid access to a wide variety of published, copyright information.

eBooks can help your research by enabling you to bookmark chapters, annotate text and use instant searches to find specific words or phrases. Several eBook files would fit on even a small laptop or PDA.

NEW: Save money by eSubscribing: cheap, online access to any eBook for as long as you need it.

Annual subscription packages

We now offer special low-cost bulk subscriptions to packages of eBooks in certain subject areas. These are available to libraries or to individuals.

For more information please contact webmaster.ebooks@tandf.co.uk

We're continually developing the eBook concept, so keep up to date by visiting the website.

www.eBookstore.tandf.co.uk